The Land and People of
CUBA

The island of Cuba was described by Columbus, the first European to explore it, as a tropical paradise. As its natural riches were exploited by subsequent settlers, colonial Cuba became a focus for rivalry between other nations. The Republic of Cuba, brought to its present form by a revolution in 1959, is among the more controversial areas of the world today.

This book presents an account of Cuban history in which recent events are shown to be part of a pattern traceable to the earliest confrontations between Indians and Europeans. The author explores many of the policies, both domestic and international, that have made Cuba such a center of controversy, and describes the way of life of the Cuban people.

PORTRAITS OF THE NATIONS SERIES

Also in the same format

The Land and People of
CUBA

by Victoria Ortiz

PORTRAITS OF THE NATIONS SERIES

J. B. LIPPINCOTT COMPANY
Philadelphia   New York

U.S. Library of Congress Cataloging in Publication Data

Ortiz, Victoria, birth date
  The land and people of Cuba.

  (Portraits of the nations series)
  SUMMARY: The history of Cuba from its discovery in the fifteenth century
by early explorers to the present day.
  1. Cuba—History—Juvenile literature. [1. Cuba—History] I. Title.
F1758.5.O77   917.291′03′064   72-11878
ISBN-0-397-31382-9

Map by Donald T. Pitcher

To Dinah, without whom . . .

Contents

The Land and People of
CUBA

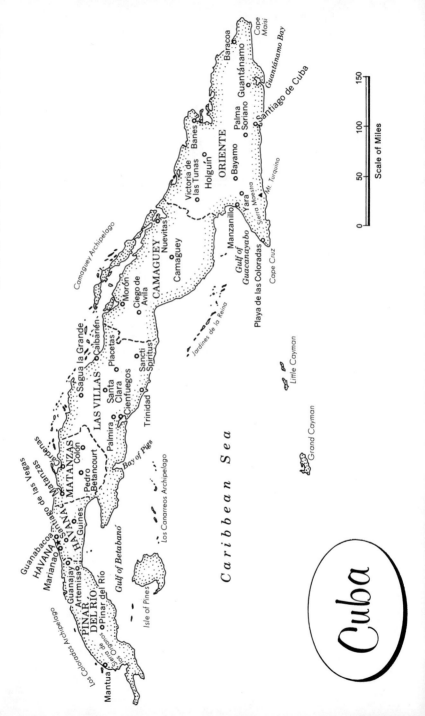

Gulf of Mexico

ATLANTIC OCEAN

Caribbean Sea

Cuba

Scale of Miles
0 50 100 150

Prologue

Genesis of a Revolution

"We were much weakened after a march more arduous than long. On December 2 [1956] we had landed in a place called Playa de las Coloradas, losing almost all our equipment and walking for endless hours through salt-water marshes. We all wore new boots which had blistered our feet. But our footwear and the resulting fungal infections were not our only enemies. We had left the Mexican port of Tuxpan on November 25, a day on which the north wind . . . made navigation hazardous. We landed in Cuba after seven days of crossing the Gulf of Mexico and the Caribbean. We sailed without food, our boat was in poor repair, and most of us, unused to sea travel, were seasick. All this had left its mark on the troop of rookies who had never known combat. . . ."

This was the beginning of the Cuban Revolution, as described by Che Guevara. That the revolution today is in its second decade, and the socialist government of Cuba is reasonably stable, is extraordinary in the light of such an inauspicious start. Here we have eighty-two men, tired, ill, inexperienced, lost, ingenuously resting in a cane field and visible to Batista's planes circling above them. That such a small force, with such a vague understanding of how to wage

11

The swamp at Playa de las Coloradas, where the rebels landed in December, 1956.

guerrilla warfare, should succeed two years later in defeating the sophisticated government army and in becoming the new government of Cuba is surprising.

More surprising, perhaps, to the outside observer, is the fact that the island of Cuba—tiny by comparison to its neighbors—has so often been a cause for concern, speculation, argument, criticism, and praise in the United States and in other countries. Cuba has been variously referred to as a "prophetic island," a "tragedy in our hemisphere," a "Communist menace," and "the free territory of America." What is it about Cuba that has caused it to be the catalyst for such impassioned thought and discussion? Why has this small island brought so many sleepless nights to her own leaders and to the leaders of other nations? Why has this tropical paradise been seen by some as the herald of continental doom, and by others as the harbinger of a new and better life for all Americans? Only an examination of Cuba's history can hope to explain to us what has happened there since those bearded men landed at Playa de las Coloradas.

Cuba's geography has played a major role in the development of its political character. From the earliest days of Spanish domination, Cuba's strategic location straddling the Gulf of Mexico placed it in a position of prime military and political importance. In its early days as a Spanish colony, Cuba was a pawn in the constant struggles among the major European powers for control of the New World. In later years, when this rivalry had narrowed down to one between Spain and the United States, the tiny island once again assumed major proportions from a strategic point of view. And with the advent of the Cuban Revolution in 1959, its closeness to the United States (ninety-two miles south of Key West, Florida) provided a focal point for North American opposition to the Castro government.

Cuba's natural physical characteristics have been both ally and enemy of whatever group was fighting for dominance. For the early settlers the fine harbors were a blessing, since the Spanish fleet used the ports as supply points on the long voyage between Spain and the New World; but they were also frequently the targets of pirates, buccaneers, and enemy navies during the European wars. The Sierra Maestra—Cuba's only major mountain range, in the eastern part of the island—provided natural asylum for escaping Indians and African slaves; the sierra was the site of many of the battles fought during the war for independence from Spain; and in the late 1950s these mountains were the point from which the revolutionary forces launched the assaults which eventually won them the island.

The configuration of Cuba's population, and the various needs and interests of each group in the society, have their origins in the first contacts between the Indians and the Spaniards. We shall see that the kind of relations which were established as early as 1492 set the pattern for future social interaction. What happened between the "discoverers" and the original Cubans was soon to be mirrored in relations between masters and slaves, between the Spanish imperial government and the growing Cuban Creole population, between landowners and peasants, and ultimately between the United States and Cuba.

Let us return, then, to those years in the late fifteenth and early sixteenth centuries when the Western world reached the tiny tropical island of Cuba and confronted her original inhabitants with those earliest carriers of civilization, the conquistador and the priest.

1

Two Worlds Meet

*We do not know on what account they come,
but we know the Spaniards are cruel and wicked
people.*

Chief Hatuey

While Europeans were arguing the question of the earth's shape, on the other side of the globe civilizations were thriving. Although nowhere near as highly developed as either the Aztecs and Mayas of Mexico and Central America or the Incas of Peru, the Indians of Cuba formed a well-structured society of chiefdoms, whose main economic activities were agriculture and fishing.

The Indians whom Columbus saw when he landed in Cuba were the Arawak Taínos, whose greater advancement had permitted them to displace the Guanajatabeyes and the Ciboneyes. While these latter groups were paleolithic civilizations—using only crude stone implements, as well as some of shell and fish bone—the Taínos are classified as neolithic. Their tools were of polished stone and carved wood, and their agriculture was more highly developed. Fertilizing their fields with urine and wood ash, they grew maize, potatoes, beans, arrowroot, and peppers. And they knew how to harvest what nature provided so abundantly: avocados, papayas, coconuts, and peanuts.

Of all the crops grown by the Taínos, there is one which was perhaps the most important in terms of its effect on future civilizations: tobacco. Columbus noted that the Indians he met smoked dried, rolled leaves (cigars) "with which their bodies became benumbed and they were as if intoxicated, and it was said that in this way they did not feel tired."

The island has never provided much natural game, so the Taíno diet was somewhat restricted in terms of meat. The great delicacies, reserved for the chief or *cacique,* were the agouti, a small rodent, and the iguana, a large lizard. The rest of the people had to make do with small birds, reptiles, spiders, worms, and insects to supplement their diet of vegetables, fish, and shellfish. This sparseness of wild fauna also limited the number of domesticated animals the Taínos had. There were two that we know of, the hunting bird and a curious species of mute dog. These dogs were seen in Indian huts by Columbus, who mentioned on several occasions "dogs which do not bark."

The Taínos lived in huts or *bohíos* which have changed little from earlier times and may still be seen in Cuba. They are small, round, one-roomed dwellings with cone-shaped roofs of palm leaves. The chiefs lived in more lavish structures: large, rectangular houses with thatched roofs. While the commoners slept in hammocks of twisted cotton and had no other furnishings beyond their gourds and working and cooking utensils, the chiefs and their families slept on platform beds and owned stone or carved wood stools.

Taíno caciques inherited their position, although in the absence of an appropriate heir the people could elect one. The position was an important one, since the chief had control of virtually all aspects of village life: he distributed surplus crops, mediated arguments, led religious festivities, hosted visiting dignitaries, and often served also as priest or shaman. His political power was derived primarily from the supernatural powers of his *zemis* or gods. Taíno religion was based on a rather complex system of zemis who controlled both natural and spiritual forces. Each person might own a number of zemis, and as long as he owned them they worked for him. But since the zemis were housed in idols of clay, wood, cotton, bone, and gold, they could be stolen and their power passed on to their new owners.

The zemis took different forms, just as they had different powers. Most often they took the shapes of animals, although they also appeared as grotesque humanoid figures with exaggerated sexual organs. Each zemi had its own symbols, and the wealthier Taínos often painted these symbols on their bodies and carved them into their household implements. The most powerful zemis, those owned by the chief, were safely housed in special temples on the outskirts of the village; when the cacique faced a major decision he went to his zemis' temple and through taking a hallucinogenic snuff would receive the zemis' pronouncements.

The village shaman or doctor also had zemis, and these he used to cure the sick and wounded. Should the cure not work, the family of the deceased Taíno might beat the shaman, but they never killed him, fearing his great powers. When he recovered from the beating, this was seen as further proof of his zemis' strength, for it would be said that his zemi had taken the form of a snake and had licked the evil out of his wounds.

Agricultural and religious activities were what most occupied the Taínos. They were not a warlike people, as Columbus noted on several occasions, and managed to maintain hegemony on the island by means other than war. If, however, war was unavoidable, all the men fought, painting their bodies red and wearing miniature stone zemis. They used primitive weapons—spears, spear throwers, clubs, javelins, and stones—and relied primarily on their tactics which involved ambushes and surprise attacks. As we shall see, the Indians were able to keep the Spanish invaders at bay for quite a time by using these methods of jungle warfare, although eventually they were defeated by the Spanish soldiers.

As the Taínos went about their simple lives, in Spain Columbus was planning a voyage which would not only shatter Taíno society but would also have resounding effects throughout the known world. On August 2, 1492, Columbus and his men sailed from Spain with three ships. Their destination was "the Indies," which were later to be known as the New World. Columbus was particularly anxious to find the large island of Cipangu which he had heard about from other navigators. He hoped to find great wealth there, and then to proceed to the mainland of Cathay and the riches spoken of by Marco Polo.

On Friday, October 12, Columbus and his men reached the New World, and as early as October 24 they began to hear talk of a large island not far off, reputed to be rich in gold and spices and active in shipping and trading. It is not difficult to imagine Columbus's disappointment when he finally reached "Cathay" and found only unclad Indians and very little gold.

Since Columbus was seeing land which had not previously been charted, it is sometimes difficult in reading his journals to determine which island he landed on and when. However, it becomes clear as his journeys progress that the island he named Juana is today's Cuba. He landed there October 28, and was awed by the natural beauty of the island and very much taken by the friendliness of the inhabitants.

Although Columbus "discovered" Cuba in 1492, it was not until 1511 that the first Spanish settlement was established there. The neighboring island of Hispaniola (today shared by Haiti and the Dominican Republic) was the first Caribbean island to be settled, in 1496.

Initially the Cuban Taínos were ready to welcome the Spanish visitors, but by 1511 they had communicated with Indians on Hispaniola and had been warned of the dangers of Spanish settlement. The Spaniards, whose main interest in the New World was the conquest of territory and of gold, were little concerned with the lives of the original inhabitants. As they moved through the area, the Spaniards enslaved the Indians and put them to work in the gold mines. Working under harsh conditions, many Indians died, while others fled to the mountains.

The best-known Indian leader of the early period of settlement (early 1500s) was young Hatuey, chieftain of the island of Guahaba, near Haiti. The Spaniards had landed there before they reached Cuba, and Hatuey had refused to see Columbus, having heard how brutally the newcomers treated the Indians. With his whole village Hatuey planned to resist, but the invaders' superior strength forced him to lead his people to safety in the mountains.

After the first defeat, Hatuey took the four hundred survivors of his village and in canoes they sailed to Cuba, which had been visited but not yet settled by Spain. Once in Cuba, Hatuey gathered the Taíno chiefs together and after explaining to them what the Spaniards had already done, he pleaded with them to join his people and expel any Spaniard who might land there. But the Taínos were fearful of Hatuey's people, and not all the chiefs trusted the impetuous young leader.

Knowing that the Spaniards would soon land, Hatuey and his men, joined by a few Taínos, hid themselves behind trees and rocks along the beach and awaited the arrival of their enemy. Led by Diego Velásquez, Hernán Cortés (who went on to conquer the Aztec Empire in Mexico), and Francisco de Morales, the Spaniards landed and were greeted by a hail of arrows. Although several invaders were wounded, the Indians sustained many more casualties, and Hatuey was forced to retreat with his followers. Once again he appealed to the Taíno chiefs to help him against the Spaniards; the Taínos still mistrusted Hatuey more than they did the newcomers, and once more refused to help.

Despite the caciques' refusal, Hatuey's forces were joined by quite a few Taíno warriors, and soon they outnumbered the Spanish troops in their fort at Baracoa. The Indians were able to keep going for three months by using tactics not unlike what today is called guerrilla warfare: they were past masters at surprise attacks, ambushes, and general military harassment. And these tactics brought some results, for the Spaniards had not encountered such resistance in Hispaniola. Locked up in their fort, badgered constantly by an invisible enemy, the Spaniards began to lose their spirit, and some dissension broke out among them as the siege continued.

But the Spanish troops had two vital advantages over the Indians: horses and gunpowder. Hatuey's defeat was inevitable, and was merely hastened when an Indian betrayed him to the soldiers, who immediately captured him. Although the Spaniards promised Hatuey his life if he would tell them where his people had hidden their gold, he refused, and on February 2, 1512, Hatuey was burned at the stake. His death was closely followed by the total collapse of Indian resistance; some of Hatuey's men were captured, branded on the forehead, and then enslaved. The remaining Indians quietly gave in.

Uprisings against the Spaniards did, however, continue sporadically for several years. In 1529 the Indian Guama and his wife Habaguanex, both born in Cuba, led a sizable uprising, launching assaults against the Spaniards from the mountains in eastern Cuba. But by 1532 the Spanish army had again triumphed, and this was the last major organized Indian revolt.

Having established themselves as rulers of Cuba, the Spaniards proceeded with the more important business of finding gold. They organized expeditions into the interior of the island and took with them priests, whose job was the conversion of Indian souls. On many of these trips the soldiers were accompanied by Father Bartolomé de las Casas, soon to become the most impassioned and articulate defender of the Indian. On these early expeditions the father witnessed the barbarities of the Spaniards against the Indians, writing later, "No one can describe vividly enough the villainous acts perpetrated by these brutal men. They appear to have declared themselves enemies of all men."

Las Casas has chronicled for posterity incident upon incident of Spanish villainy. During the expeditions in search of gold, friendly villagers would offer food and water to the Spaniards. After refreshing themselves, the soldiers turned upon their hosts and slaughtered entire villages.

The genocide did not stop with the establishment of Spanish settlements. Indian lands were expropriated, native labor enslaved, resisters beaten and tortured, and women raped. Las Casas reported that during a period of three or four months he saw thousands of children die of starvation, because their parents had been forced to work in the mines and they had no one to feed them. The record of Spanish atrocities includes such acts as hunting Indians as if they were animals, testing the sharpness of swords by beheading Indians, and feeding Indians to dogs. On every occasion that Las Casas and others described such barbarities to the Spanish Crown or to its representative in the empire, the reports were scoffed at as exaggerated.

As the Spanish colony in Cuba grew, more organized methods for subduing the Indians were developed. Best known of these was the *encomienda,* a system whereby Indians were forced to work for the Spaniards in return for "protection" and conversion to Catholicism. The encomienda system was not legal slavery, an institution to be introduced later, but in fact no Indian had a choice in the matter.

The imposition of Spanish values and institutions was in total contradiction to what the Indians had known before. Among the Taínos there was no notion of individually owned land, even where the cacique was concerned. Lands were either held communally or cultivated by large family groups. In all cases, the surplus crop was distributed by the cacique to benefit all members of the village. There was no concept of buying and selling land, or of having exclusive rights to it. The advent of the Spanish economic system was a death blow, literally and figuratively, to Indian society.

While there were Spaniards who protested the treatment of the Indians, most of these protests were ineffectual since the entire Spanish community depended on the land and labor of the Indians. Little was done of any substance to better the lot of the Indian, and it was only in 1559, by the time most of the Indian population had died off, that the encomienda system was officially abolished, to be replaced by African slavery, a system of greater proportions and greater inhumanity. How else would the settlers be able to colonize and cultivate this Caribbean gem, this tiny island paradise which offered them so many riches?

2

Pearl of the Antilles

This is the most beautiful land my eyes have ever seen.

Christopher Columbus

Upon first landing in Cuba, the visitor is struck by the island's natural beauty. Columbus was the first to note this for posterity, declaring that he had never seen a land as lovely. His journals and his chroniclers tell us of his amazement before the natural wonders of the Cuban landscape; at one point he was so entranced by the melodious singing of the birds that he asserted his unwillingness ever to leave.

Columbus was of course well prepared to find Cuba exotic and dazzling, for when he landed there he believed that he had finally reached Cathay, the mysterious Oriental land described by Marco Polo. Not until sixteen years later was Cuba found in fact to be an island.

Let us share with Columbus that first glimpse of Cuba, for the centuries have not changed it very much. He anchored in the mouth of a river and noted many different trees in the vicinity, none of

Tropical vegetation typical of the island's interior.

which were familiar to him and all of which bore flowers of bright
and extravagant colors. He exclaimed on the variety of fruits borne
by these trees—and today we know that he was seeing for the first
time, and no doubt tasting, pineapples, coconuts, and papayas.

As he sailed along the coast, still believing of course that it was the
mainland, he noted the marvelous natural harbors; and on seeing that
the vegetation descended almost to the shore, he realized that the sea

must not be very stormy, and this made the coastal region even more attractive to him.

In the evenings, as these early Spaniards sat on the beaches, they rejoiced in the cooling breezes and enjoyed the clean and flower-scented air. Even in the interior, as they explored further, Columbus and his men were continually amazed by the temperate climate (which they compared nostalgically to that of Andalucía in the spring), the fresh winds, and the lush vegetation.

Columbus also observed the mountains, several very high peaks and few ranges, and found the plains of the interior pleasing and potential pastures for the raising of livestock. From his few conversations with the Indians on the island he learned that there were ample rivers inland, supplying fresh water and irrigating the fields.

The modern visitor to Cuba would see more or less what Columbus saw. The island is a botanist's delight, boasting over eight thousand species of trees and plants. Flowers are abundant and of brilliant gemlike colors. The merit of the island's topography was well understood by Columbus. Cuba is in fact one large plain, with a cluster of largish mountains in the east and a few smaller ones in the interior and the west. The central part of the island is softly landscaped by small plains and shallow valleys. There are over two hundred small rivers and streams, and while there is no major river, the lesser ones provide ample irrigation and drinking water, except for periods during the dry winter months.

Cuba's climate is indeed temperate. Classified as subtropical, the temperature is rarely higher than eighty degrees and drops no lower than seventy degrees. The gentle trade winds cool the coastal regions, and in the interior the crisscrossing breezes provide relief from the noonday sun. The rainfall is even throughout the island, and although quite heavy in the rainy season, only occasionally grows to storm proportions. Cuba's eastern coast is perhaps less lucky than the rest of the island, for it is often the target of hurricanes during the months of August, September, and October.

As Columbus noted, Cuba is also rich in natural harbors, and the major port cities—Havana, Santiago, Baracoa—are located in the precise spots which the early Spaniards had chosen for the first primitive ports they built. In fact, even the early settlements in the interior were so well situated by the Spaniards that today's provincial capitals are all on more or less the same sites.

Columbus was shortsighted in one way. While he admired Cuba's physical beauties, he did not foresee their worth. When the Spaniards did not find as much gold as they expected, nor jewels and rich spices, they chose to look elsewhere, and Cuba remained for many years no more than a sort of halfway point between Europe and more lucrative regions in Mexico and Peru. It was only later that Cuba's "gold" and "jewels"—sugar and tobacco—were discovered and exploited.

Thus, Cuba was settled haphazardly and slowly. No one took very seriously the idea of building permanent settlements for residential purposes until much later. At first the most important structures built were the forts to protect the harbors. In Havana the Morro Castle remains to this day as a memory of those early times when piracy and invasion by rival European powers constantly plagued the few Spanish residents of the island. The hundreds of keys and smaller islands surrounding Cuba were virtually ignored, except perhaps in terms of their defense value. Only later did the Isle of Pines attract small groups of charcoal makers, as well as fishermen who chose to live isolated there, finding their livelihood from the riches offered by the sea: fish, crustaceans, and sponges.

As time went on, however, more and more Spaniards decided to stay on the island, and certain of Cuba's natural resources began to be cultivated. The sugar industry grew rapidly after the development of the slave trade, and the plains which had so impressed Columbus were indeed used for the raising of cattle. And so the cities grew, for the pattern of Spanish agriculture was such that the large landowners preferred to live in cities, away from their lands; and those large plantations, being worked eventually by slaves imported from Africa, provided little or no work for the growing population of *guajiros* or peasants, who then also migrated to the cities in search of work.

Physically, then, Cuba has always been a land of great variety and great contrasts. This variety is mirrored in the population. We have seen that the first true Cubans were the Guanajatabey, the Ciboney, and the Taíno Indians, and that with the coming of the Spaniards their cultures and their population were virtually destroyed. There are few traces today of the sixty thousand Taínos who inhabited Cuba in 1492, although quite recently a Cuban anthropologist discovered, in a remote area of Oriente Province, a small group of families who physically and culturally show traits of these early civilizations. In all social respects, however, they are not Indian; they speak Spanish and live much as their neighbors do.

Recent Cuban postage stamps depict the island's diverse fauna.

It is difficult to ascribe an ethnic structure to Cuba because, like most Latin-American countries, Cuba is today a country of people of mixed origins: mulattoes (black and Spanish), mestizos (Indian and Spanish), and *criollos* or Creoles (Cuban-born Spaniards, and, later, Cuban-born blacks). For a long time it was considered a mark of social distinction to claim direct, unsullied Spanish lineage, and many of the wealthiest Cuban families protested that all of their marriages had been with others of pure Spanish blood. Realistically, though, it cannot be maintained that there are any true Spaniards in Cuba, beyond those who came in the late 1930s as refugees from Franco's Spain, and a few others. "Pure-blooded" Spaniards are in fact Creoles.

Another group that went to Cuba to escape political turmoil in Europe was the Irish. During the Battle of the Boyne (1690) many Irish chose Cuba because it was a Catholic country. Many prominent members of the Spanish army were Irish, and to this day there are Cubans named O'Lawlor, O'Reilly, O'Farrell, and O'Donnell.

Cubans of French origin are descended from the wealthy planters who fled Haiti during the slave uprising there (1791–1797) and came to Cuba bringing French culture and customs and, most important, the coffee plant. Coffee subsequently became second in importance only to sugar and tobacco.

Members of other national and ethnic groups, in more recent times, have left their own countries for political or religious reasons and have settled in Cuba. Just as the Spaniards came during the Spanish Civil War, so many European Jews settled there when they fled Hitler. There is a substantial Jewish community, primarily in Havana, which has not mingled much with the rest of the Cuban population. The Jews have worked mostly in small businesses and have also been active in the trade unions.

The settlement in Cuba of various national groups has not seriously affected the language, and Spanish has been spoken in Cuba ever since the first European settlements were established. It is important to note, however, that Cuban Spanish has always been liberally sprinkled with terminology brought by the slaves from Africa.

Despite the clear supremacy of Spanish, from the beginning of this century English has more or less been the second language in Cuba because of the influence of the United States on the island. English was and is the major foreign language taught in Cuban schools. From the early 1940s until 1959, thousands of tourists visited Cuba from the United States all year long, bringing not only their language but their customs and tastes as well. Before 1959, when the United States still had business interests and diplomatic personnel in Cuba, there was a large North American community there. Along with the British and Canadians living and working in Cuba, they were known as the ABC's. Since 1959, of course, the number of ABC's has diminished sharply, although there is still a small community of English-speaking residents.

Most national or ethnic groups have come to Cuba by choice and have settled there quite comfortably to pursue their various styles of living. The major ethnic strain in the Cuban population, however, originates in a group which was brought to the island by force in the early sixteenth century, to live and work there under the most inhuman of conditions. Ethnically, culturally, artistically, and above all economically, the African slaves imported to Cuba, and their black and mulatto descendants, have profoundly affected the course of the island's history.

3

Masters and Slaves

Life is cheap, and sugar, sir—is gold.

Juan Francisco Manzano

With the virtually total destruction of the Indian population the Spanish colonists in Cuba were frantic to find other people to work their mines and fields. By the end of the fifteenth century the slave trade had developed among the European nations, and it was not long before the colonists began importing African slaves from Spain. As early as 1513, in fact, the Spanish Crown issued a permit allowing the importation of slaves to Cuba, and the first large group of African slaves, three hundred of them, reached Cuba in 1524. From then on the slave population of the island grew, sometimes slowly, sometimes more rapidly, depending on the parallel growth of the large sugar, tobacco, and coffee plantations. By the middle of the nineteenth century, close to 60 percent of Cuba's population was black and mulatto.

The life of a slave in Cuba differed little from that of a slave in the United States. On paper, though, and in a few real ways, Cuban slaves were slightly better off. In one especially important area,

Cuban slaves were lucky: they were allowed to own, exchange, and sell property, and to accumulate capital. This allowed for the system of *coartación,* whereby a Cuban slave could purchase his or her own freedom, or that of his or her parents or children, in installments. In addition, Cuban slaves were allowed to marry; they could request a change of masters so long as they could find a substitute willing to buy them; and children born of the union of a slave and a colonist were automatically free.

In reality, though, the lot of the slave was in no way a fortunate one. Most of the slaves had been prisoners of African chiefs who sold them to the slave traders, usually British. Already torn from their families and homes, the slaves were then loaded onto slave ships and taken many thousands of miles to a totally foreign land. On the ships conditions were, to say the least, overcrowded and unsanitary, and anywhere from 25 to 50 percent of the slaves died on the voyage to Cuba. Many more threw themselves overboard rather than face the unsure future of enslavement. On some ships there were abortive mutinies among the slaves, but despite these attempts and despite tremendous attrition, Cuba rapidly became a society built upon human slavery.

On the plantations the working life of a field slave was ten years, for work was hard, hours long, food scarce, and punishment frequent and brutal. Housed originally in *bohíos* or huts, with the increase in slave uprisings on the plantations the slaves were soon moved into large buildings called barracoons. Here lived as many as two hundred slaves—men, women, and children, each with a tiny cubicle closed off by a door which could be locked to prevent theft of whatever poor belongings they had.

The day typically began at 4:30 in the morning, when the deputy overseer would leave his own cubicle in the barracoon, unlock the large padlock on the door, and ring nine strokes on the bell—the Ave Maria—to tell the slaves to rise immediately. At 6:00 the lineup bell was rung, and the women lined up on one side, the men on the other. After roll call, both lines were marched to the fields and the workday began. At 11:00 they stopped work briefly to eat lunch

Slaves on the way to market to be sold.

—jerked beef, vegetables, and bread—and then continued their labors until the bell for prayers rang at sunset. At 8:30 the bell rang for bedtime, and the slaves were locked into the barracoon for the night.

On some less harsh plantations the rule of no work on Sunday was observed, and this became the only day for any kind of recreation. There were frequent festivals, with singing, drumming, and dancing.

Often visits to a nearby tavern were permitted, and there the men would play cards and drink *aguardiente,* a strong cane liquor (literally "burning water"). At the tavern they could also sell whatever surplus crops they had grown on the small plots allowed them for vegetables and the like. Here, too, they could purchase trinkets and could perhaps be traded to a new and more lenient master.

But recreation was rare in a situation where the slightest alleged infraction of a rule was punishable by up to four months in the stocks. There were two kinds of stocks, those for standing in and those for lying in. Both were made of heavy wooden planks, with holes for head, hands, and feet. Graver offenses were punished by whipping or flogging. The overseer was in charge of this activity, which he carried out with either a rawhide lash which left great weals on the offender's back, or with whips made of plant fibers which flayed the skin off in strips. Special arrangements were made for the beating of pregnant women: a hollow was dug in the ground, over which the woman would lie so that her abdomen rested in the hole. She was whipped harshly but with care, for each child born was a slave at no cost to the master.

Slave children were all born in the infirmary and lived there until old enough to work, usually six or seven years of age. They were cared for by wet nurses and cooks, who also looked after the sick. Since no doctors or medications were provided, these women soon became adept at the art of healing with homemade herbal remedies. Willy-nilly, they found themselves treating slaves suffering from general fatigue and malnutrition, from colic, whooping cough, measles, smallpox, or what was known as the "black sickness." For the treatment of wounds received in a whipping, they used tobacco leaves, urine, and salt.

Many slaves died of disease on the plantations, although the slaveowners made some minimal attempts to keep them well. After all, they had paid up to five hundred dollars for each slave. The slaves were issued clothing: rough linen shirts and pants for the men; blouses, skirts, and petticoats for the women. These were worn until they were literally rags, and only then were new clothes issued.

The plantation owners provided little substantial food for the slaves, and most nourished themselves and their families primarily from what they were able to grow on their tiny plots of land: sweet potatoes, gourds, okra, kidney beans, yucca, and peanuts. Some, more fortunate, were able to purchase and raise a pig.

Surprisingly enough, while the slaves' bodies were so maltreated, their cultural heritage suffered less in Cuba than in the United States. The Spanish Catholic church, by no means a seat of liberalism, seemed to understand that its teachings would be better received by the "heathen" if the poor souls were allowed simultaneously to hold onto their own religions. Throughout Latin America, we find blends of Catholicism with local Indian religions; in Cuba we see a kind of Catholicism which is often highly colored with remnants of the African religions brought there by the slaves.

Most notable of these is Santería, a group of cults which very soon included Catholicism. Still practiced today by many Afro-Cubans, Santería has developed through a clear melding of African beliefs and Christian dogma. Especially in its gods and spirits, Santería shows its closeness to Catholicism: the followers of Santería believe that the names of Christian saints are actually translations of the names of Nigerian gods. Spirits in Santería are interchangeably called *santos* or *orishas,* and each is closely linked to a Christian saint. Shango, god of war and virility, is associated, strangely, with Saint Barbara, even though she is a woman; Elegua, Master of Paths or Directions, finds his counterpart in Saint Peter, Keeper of the Gates of Heaven; Esu is the devil; Obatalá is Jesus Christ; Odudua is the Virgin Mary; and Ogún is Saint John the Baptist. Most extraordinary of all are the pictures of saints whose faces are clearly marked with tribal identification scars!

Many other cultural aspects of African life in Cuba have come down to modern times. There has long been a highly developed school of Afro-Cuban poetry which uses African themes and rhythms as its poetic sources. There is a parallel movement in the plastic arts, and African dances and music have been carefully preserved both by the people and by the National Folkloric Ballet of Cuba. Other threads of African music have found their way into the popular dance rhythms considered typically Cuban: rumba, conga, *son,* bolero, mambo, and pachanga.

Only in more recent times, however, have these contributions of the slaves and their descendants been fully appreciated in Cuba and abroad. For centuries the black Cuban was left to work out his or her life in the fields or in the houses of the plantations, or at menial tasks in the cities. When life became intolerable, many slaves committed suicide, believing that death would at last return them to their homes in Africa. Most frequently these suicides were by hanging or by poison, although many slaves choked themselves on their tongues.

Those who found slavery intolerable but life itself worthwhile escaped into the mountains and became *cimarrones,* a term also applied to the Indians who escaped from the mines. These cimarrones were often hunted by slave-catchers and bloodhounds. Some slaves

Santa Barbara with African tribal scars on her face.

fled to *palenques,* fortified settlements in the hills where they joined other escaped Africans and Indians. From here they often organized raids on nearby plantations, and participated in slave uprisings.

These were frequent during the whole period of Cuban slavery, although always unsuccessful. The first recorded slave revolt in Cuba took place in 1533 at the Jobabo mines. Only four slaves were involved, but the uprising provoked such fear among the Spanish and Creole slaveowners that the governor sent a huge armed force to put it down. The four slaves defended themselves to the death, and their heads were then displayed to calm the terrified colonists.

As the sugar industry grew, slavery grew; and as the numbers of slaves increased, their situation worsened and the colonists became more fearful. There were countless revolts, big and small, by slaves in Cuba, and by 1789 the Spanish Crown responded to the situation by passing a new law regulating the treatment of slaves on the island. Slaveowners were to clothe and feed their slaves in accordance with certain standards, and were also to provide a priest for their religious instruction. Punishment could not be too inhuman: whipping, for example, had to be limited to only twenty-five lashes. The slaves were to work at jobs appropriate to their age and sex, and could not be expected to work more than 270 days a year. Any slaveowner disobeying these regulations would be fined or would lose the slave whom he had offended.

Although more reasonable than the anarchy which had prevailed in treatment of slaves, this new law was rarely observed, except those parts of it which regulated the slaves' behavior. In fact, after 1789 the situation worsened for slaves in Cuba. This, and the slave uprising in Haiti, further sharpened the tensions between slave and master.

In 1791, led by the slave Toussaint L'Ouverture, the slaves of Haiti rose up en masse and after six years of fighting defeated the French army and expelled the French from the island, establishing the first and only black republic in the Western Hemisphere. Many of the fleeing French planters went to Cuba, bringing with them horror stories of what had happened: plantations looted and burned, planters killed, the landscape devastated. For the Creole planters of Cuba the news was dreadful, and made them fear even more their own slaves' potential for revolt.

For the Cuban slaves the events in Haiti were heartening, to say the least. Directly inspired by what happened on the neighboring island, a freed Cuban slave, Nicolás Morales, organized a network of conspirators throughout Cuba. More than a military endeavor of revenge, this movement demanded the abolition of slavery, equality between blacks and whites, the elimination of taxes to Spain, and the distribution of plantation lands to the slaves who worked them. The revolt was crushed before it began.

Not long after, however, another young free black Cuban organized a widespread conspiracy. José Antonio Aponte, a carpenter and woodcarver living in Havana, saw himself as a black Moses whose God-given mission was the freeing of the Cuban slaves. Made up of slaves and freemen, his group planned to burn all the sugar and coffee plantations on the island, thereby making slavery totally unnecessary.

A short while before the islandwide insurrection was to occur, two men were arrested when police heard them discussing the plans. They were tortured by the police and at last named Aponte as their leader. The young Moses and eight of his followers were arrested.

The arrests did not stop the uprising, however, and several plantations were in fact burned by their slaves on the appointed day. But once again the army quelled the uprising, and on April 9, 1812, hanged Aponte and his eight companions. As a lesson to others, and in order to calm the fears of the slaveowners, the army displayed Aponte's head in a metal cage which they put by the house where he had lived; his severed hand was hung up in a street nearby.

Despite the dire warnings of the government, despite increased punishment and torture for recalcitrant slaves, these insurrections continued, culminating in what is perhaps the most famous and the bloodiest: the conspiracy of La Escalera.

This plot was discovered in 1844, and it was found that for at least three years previously there had been clandestine meetings of freemen, slaves, and even some white Cubans. These meetings were for the express purpose of organizing an uprising to bring about the end of slavery and full equality of blacks and whites. As usual, the uprising was put down before it even flowered. What made this different from earlier incidents was the brutality of the government's response.

Thousands of people—slaves and freemen, Creoles and mulattoes, Cubans and foreigners—were arrested and tortured. The blacks and mulattoes, slave and free, were especially mistreated: using a technique which gave the incident its name (La Escalera—"The Ladder"), the suspects were tied to ladders and whipped viciously until they confessed. Almost one hundred persons were condemned to death, over a thousand were imprisoned, and four hundred were exiled. And no one knows exactly how many died from the torture to which they were subjected. Although all of this was done with very little proof against the victims, after it was over the authorities denied that anyone had been unjustly treated or illegally killed.

This bloody episode was important for many reasons. As noted above, the government responded more violently to the alleged conspiracy than ever before, because it felt more threatened than ever before. More important, though, was the fact that this was the first time so many slaves, mulattoes, freemen, and whites had joined in an abolitionist movement. The authorities recognized how dangerous such an alliance could be, and a year later were still arresting, imprisoning, or exiling "suspects."

As so often happens in such situations, the final blame for La Escalera was put on a foreigner, as if the ideals of abolition could only have been imported by some outside agitator. The Cuban government and the Spanish Crown were convinced that at the root of La Escalera was one David Turnbull, a British abolitionist who in 1840 had been appointed British consul in Havana. Turnbull had been expelled from the island before La Escalera, for organizing another revolt, and had been once again expelled in 1842 when he landed in Cuba with a crew of free British blacks, ostensibly to visit

British plantations there. While it is not surprising that the Cuban authorities chose to blame Turnbull and his ideas for La Escalera, his participation on any level has never been proved.

From the beginning of the nineteenth century, the slave system had been severely threatened both by the uprisings and by growing international pressures to end first the slave trade and then slavery itself. Already fearing a diminishing work force, many landowners in Cuba began importing Chinese coolies as indentured servants. Tricked into believing they were going to Spain where they would be paid and treated well, the coolies were purchased for four hundred dollars apiece and shipped to Panama, from where they went by rail and then by boat to Cuba.

Once in Cuba, the Chinese indentured servants were contracted to work for seven or eight years at a wage of four dollars a month. It was hoped by their employers, naturally, that at the end of the eight years the workers would be so much in debt that they would be forced to spend the rest of their lives working to repay them. (This same system was used in the hiring of *emancipados,* emancipated slaves.)

In fact, however, many Chinese were able to work their eight years and then return to China. Others committed suicide, organized revolts, or escaped to the cities. In Havana, especially, the Chinese population grew rapidly; by the second half of the nineteenth century over 140,000 Chinese had come to the island. In the cities the escaped indentured servants, or those who had completed their contracts but chose to remain, established small businesses, especially fruit stands and restaurants.

But increased harshness, vigilant authorities, and indentured servants did not help, and the knell for Cuban slavery was sounded in the United States, when the South lost the Civil War. Cuban planters had been looking to the slave states as allies in the struggle to maintain slavery; there was even an important movement favoring annexation to the United States, before the slave states lost to the Union forces. In 1886, slavery was abolished in Cuba.

However, society in Cuba continued for many, many years to main-

Machetero or cane cutter during the sugar harvest.

tain virtually the same structure it had when slavery was legal. The presence of such a large dark-skinned population in Cuba was immutable, and brought with it its own problems. Until recently a high premium was set on light skin color, and while interbreeding was an undeniable reality, intermixing between Cubans of lighter skin and those more clearly descended from African parentage was rare and frowned upon. With the increased influence of the United States after 1902, and Cuba's development as the playland of wealthy North Americans, racial segregation became a harsh fact, if not a legal one. The most exclusive clubs, theaters, hotels, resorts, and residential areas were unyieldingly closed to dark-skinned Cubans. In the same way, brown or black Cubans rarely reached higher levels of government or professional jobs. It has been only since 1959 that Cuba has moved rapidly toward becoming a truly open society from a racial or ethnic point of view.

It was the maintenance of black-white inequality, as well as the continued domination by Spain, that led to the growth of the movement for independence from Spain, a movement which reached cataclysmic proportions by the end of the nineteenth century. As did the question of slavery and abolition, independence divided Cuban society sharply, and the large sugar interests once again found themselves opposed by the growing Creole middle class, by free blacks and mulattoes, by slaves, and by the increasing peasant population.

4

The Calm and the Storm

*Hurricane, hurricane, I feel your approach
and in your gust embraced
I eagerly draw my breath. . . .*

José María de Heredia

Life in colonial Cuba was not merely a series of military expeditions against renegade Taíno Indians; nor was every Cuban directly involved in the nefarious trade in human flesh. While Indians were being massacred inland, and slaves being brought from Africa and worked to death on plantations, the population of criollos (native-born Cubans) and *peninsulares* (Spanish-born Cubans) was involved in making a comfortable life for itself.

The earliest *peninsulares* were Spanish soldiers and priests; the former came to find gold for their monarch, the latter to save souls for their church. These carriers of European culture were largely responsible for the cities which even today grace the small island of Cuba. The cities of Havana, Santiago, Guanabacoa, Trinidad, and Cienfuegos date from the sixteenth, seventeenth, and eighteenth centuries, and retain today some of the spirit of the early colonial period. They are rich in churches and cathedrals; one of the loveliest is the Cathedral of the Virgin Mary of the Immaculate Conception in Havana. Built of native limestone, which gives it its bright, almost white color, this temple was constructed by the Jesuits in 1704. The façade, ornately Tuscan, is flanked by two bell towers, different in size and shape. In each tower is a musical bell, both cast in the late seventeenth century. In 1777 bones purported to be those of Christopher Columbus were buried there and were not removed until after the Spanish-American War, at which time they were discovered to belong to another man named Columbus!

Cities and towns founded in the early colonial centuries are usually well-fortified, especially those on the coast. The Morro Castles or forts in Santiago and Havana are living reminders of the days when Cuba was frequently the target for marauding pirates and buccaneers; today their turrets provide spectacular panoramic vistas of the unbelievably blue waters of the Caribbean in one direction, and of the gleaming cities which they protected in another. In these cities many of the oldest buildings and streets remain. The streets are often narrow and cobbled, the avenues wide and palm-lined; in the center of town one generally finds a plaza framing a wrought iron bandstand, and surrounded by colonnaded sidewalks and municipal buildings or churches.

The streets and buildings make it possible to imagine life in the early days of the colony. At least for the wealthy, life was easy, unless a raiding party of smugglers or buccaneers was in town. Generally the families who decided to settle in Cuba to make a living, and who succeeded at it, led lives of leisure and comfort. In their palaces —marble-floored and staircased, wood-paneled, and porcelain-tiled —the rich of the cities wafted gently through each day, from their light and elegant breakfasts of oranges and coffee—taken in the sun-drenched, sumptuous, statue-studded gardens—through their visits to morning mass, their early afternoon siestas, and their evenings of driving in carriages to visit friends, shopping in the center of town, stopping at the plaza to listen to the band concert. The rich made lavish use of their means in order to live comfortably.

Since gold had not been plentiful in Cuba, it was not for several centuries that this well-to-do population really grew. During the first couple of centuries of the colony, these few wealthy families were primarily involved in cattle raising, an activity which Columbus had predicted would flourish on Cuba's fertile plains. As the island became richer and more populous, and as its importance in the world community increased, Cuba became a pawn in the vicissitudes of European power politics. And her population—slave and master, rich and poor, criollo and *peninsular*—was dragged willy-nilly into a turmoil which was to end with the war for independence.

In the earliest days of the colony, the settlers in Cuba had virtually

Colonial Havana harbor under siege.

complete power to rule those areas which they conquered and settled. As the colony grew, however, Spain began to impose certain restrictions, and soon insisted that all Cuban affairs were ultimately under the control of the Crown. It was Spanish government officials who divided Indian lands among the early colonists, and who also regulated the encomienda system (the distribution of Indian laborers). These officials, under orders from Spain, established rigid property qualifications for the colonists' participation in local affairs. The Catholic church gave full support to government decrees, and only secondarily concerned itself with providing certain social services—orphanages, hospitals, and a few primitive schools.

Little of a constructive nature was done for those who chose to settle in Cuba. Spain's major interest lay on the mainland, in the mines and fields of Mexico and Peru. For the Crown, Cuba's main value lay in its strategic position at the mouth of the Gulf of Mexico. Even this advantage was not fully recognized for almost a century. While Havana and Santiago were essential stopover points on the long voyages between Spain and the New World, they were poorly governed and only minimally fortified. The ports were often subjected to attacks by foreign powers and by pirates. During periods of war in Europe, the ports were on occasion invaded and occupied by the ships of enemy nations; during periods of relative peace it was the privateers and buccaneers, sub rosa representatives of other countries, who harassed the island.

The pirates, mostly French, Portuguese, and Dutch, were interested in any booty of value, and preyed on the ships returning from Mexico laden with gold and spices. In 1553 the French privateer François Le Clerc, known as Timberleg, launched a campaign of pillaging and burning port towns with his ten French warships. In 1554 he took Santiago, and the following year Jacques Sores, his lieutenant, captured Havana with two ships and burned it to the ground. On each such occasion, the inhabitants of the port towns had no other recourse than to flee to the hills and then return to rebuild their settlements. Finally, in the mid-sixteenth century, Spain devised a more sophisticated fleet system designed to protect its Caribbean commerce, and saw fit to fortify Cuban ports. Because of Havana's increasing importance as a supply stop, the city was declared the island's capital in 1589, and along with the other towns was from then on governed by military men with the title of Governor-General. Fortifications were built and the number of soldiers increased. As the island's capital, Havana grew rapidly, and by 1762 boasted a population of close to forty thousand, making it the third largest city in the New World, more populous at the time than Boston or New York.

Until the eighteenth century Cuba prospered slowly and unspectacularly. Only during the 1800s did the island begin to move more rapidly to prominence. By this period piracy had decreased, and there was an influx of Spanish colonists from Jamaica and Spain. These settlers brought with them new crops, tobacco and sugar, and initiated what was soon to become Cuba's major economic activity. The cattle ranches were broken up so that more land would be available for these new crops, and in general the economy flourished.

As the island became more prosperous, the Crown imposed more repressive trade regulations. Spain maintained a complete monopoly on tobacco exports, for example, and was unwavering in its severe taxation and tariff policies. The pattern for conflict on the island was set in those days: some Cubans, the wealthier *peninsulares,* welcomed Spanish restrictions for they benefitted from them; and others, wealthy criollos, sought freer trade and fewer restrictions. In the mid-eighteenth century the Seven Years' War between Britain and France, with Spain allied to France, opened up a new era for Cuba. In 1762 the British captured Havana and held it for ten months. During that period Cuba prospered, for trade regulations were liberalized and, best of all, the British colonies in North America were opened up to Cuban commerce. This was the beginning of a long and tumultuous relationship between Cuba and its neighbor to the north.

When the British were expelled from Cuba by Spain, some of the more liberal policies instituted by the occupying forces were main-

View of modern Havana.

tained, for Spain, too, was going through a period of relative enlightenment. Cubans could now trade with the Spanish colonies as
well as with the mother country, and the thirteen colonies, newly
independent, became a major market for coffee and sugar. Political
and intellectual life expanded also, as Cuba was finally exposed to
the liberal philosophical and social ideas which were becoming so
popular in Europe. By the end of the eighteenth century Cuba saw
the growth of formal and informal groups which championed the
concept of public education, and the revitalization of its university.

One of the most active of these groups, the Sociedad Económica,
for a long time shaped Cuban intellectual life. Founded in 1793,
the Sociedad undertook to encourage widespread education and even

financed the establishment of two public schools, one for boys and, surprisingly enough, one for girls. The group also took over the only existing newspaper, and in twenty years it grew from a weekly to a daily. The profits from the paper were used to start a library, the first in Cuba; the editorial policy of the paper was based on the continued encouragement of high educational standards and enlightened social and political philosophies.

Despite the extremely liberal stance of the Sociedad Económica and many like-minded Cubans, there developed in Cuban intellectual circles a disturbing paradox. While urging less restrictive trade practices and more individual intellectual freedoms, these men also stood staunchly against the abolition of slavery. They were strengthened in their position by the events in Haiti which culminated in 1801 when Toussaint expelled the French and declared Haiti independent and all its slaves free. The wealthy French planters who fled to Cuba merely confirmed the Cuban planters in their fears of slave uprisings, and solidified their determination to uphold the slave system in Cuba. Thus, the liberals who fought for free public education and for a free press also worked for the maintenance of the slave economy. While they wanted free trade with the rest of the Spanish empire and with the newly created North American republic, they also wanted freedom to import slaves so that the already wealthy planters might be further enriched.

A strong interest in free trade with the United States developed rapidly in the late eighteenth and early nineteenth centuries. For one thing, the young northern republic was hungry for the products so plentifully grown in Cuba—sugar, tobacco, coffee; for another, the Cubans recognized the value of and need for North American imports, clothing and food. And most important, perhaps, there were those Cubans, principally *peninsulares,* who agitated for annexation to the United States in the hope that thereby the slave system would be saved.

In spite of greater prosperity, therefore, Cuba began to feel a greater insecurity; the important and growing class of rich planters sought freedom from Spain's capricious and shifting position on trade restrictions, but wanted to maintain tight controls on the slavery question. Added to this was the fact that the slave population had increased tremendously in Cuba (from thirty-three thousand in 1790 to ninety-one thousand in 1805), and the planters, criollos and *peninsulares* alike, feared more slave uprisings and the eventual numerical superiority of the black population. As the white and wealthy classes demanded more economic and individual rights for themselves, there was the danger that the dark-skinned and poor classes might be impertinent enough to seek these rights for themselves also.

The contradictions colored Cuban political life until the end of the war for independence, and even after. The inability to fully agree on all issues meant that even by the early nineteenth century the Cuban liberals and those organizing for independence were held back from effective political action. By the late 1820s only Cuba and Puerto Rico remained as Spanish colonies in the New World, for the other members of the empire had fought for and won their independence. Cuba, referred to as the ever-faithful isle, was so caught up in its own internal conflicts that the early wars for independence passed it by. As the Spanish Crown lost its grip in the New World, it hung on even more forcefully to what was left, and the Cuban population was subjected to increasingly despotic colonial governments. These culminated in the bitter years of Governor Tacón's rule (1834–1838), which finally turned the tide in the Cuban movement for independence.

After Tacón's tenure, the political picture in Cuba became clearer. The *peninsulares* were by then mostly officials, military personnel, high government functionaries, aristocratic landholders and slaveowners, and native-born Cubans sympathetic to Spanish rule; they were dedicated to maintaining Spanish dominance on the island, and even organized a paramilitary spy group known as the Volunteers who collaborated actively with the Spanish police and army. On the other side were the criollos, more and more the leaders of the movements for reform and independence. They came from the ranks of native-born teachers, professionals, and writers, and were often joined by free blacks and slaves. While the *peninsulares* almost unanimously supported the continuance of Spanish rule, the criollos were divided into two groups: one favored freedom from Spain but the maintenance of slavery, perhaps through annexation to the United States; the other favored freedom from Spain and freedom of all Cubans from any form of enslavement.

Toward the middle of the nineteenth century the confrontations among these groups, and the frequent clashes between the *independentistas* and the Crown, only unleashed the storm which the previous epochs had heralded. Surrounded by wars and revolutions for independence—in France, Haiti, the United States, Mexico, Argentina, Peru, and the rest of Latin America—and gnawed by internal strife and discontent, Cuba soon took its place among the emerging republics seeking autonomy and freedom from foreign interference. The chronicle of Cuba's struggle for independence, and its encounter with a power even more potent than Spain, is best understood by examining the life and thinking of one of Cuba's greatest and most dedicated patriots, José Martí.

5

Titans, Apostles, and Other Patriots

My sling is that of David.

José Martí

It would be safe to assume that even in the turbulence of the last couple of centuries, few persons can be said truly to have lived history. Among all those great figures we read of as being shapers of world destiny, there cannot be many whose first enmeshment with the political forces of their time began at the age of sixteen. José Julián Martí y Pérez, beloved today as one of Cuba's and Latin America's greatest men, was such an individual; virtually every breath taken in his forty-two years of life was drawn in his involvement with the Cuban struggle for independence. Literally a child of his times, the fabric of Martí's life and thought was woven with the threads of conflict and enlightenment which so characterized the nineteenth century in Cuba.

As we have seen, by the 1820s only Cuba and Puerto Rico remained in what was once the glorious Spanish empire in the New World. Spain, crushed by massive defeats at the hand of criollos and Indians throughout Latin America, was anxious to retain power, if only symbolic, in this hemisphere. While seeing the need for some reforms in the administration of the island, the Crown was more interested in securing the loyalty of the most powerful and wealthy groups there, and little was done to improve social and political conditions for the majority of the Cuban people. As a direct result of Spanish shortsightedness, the ongoing polarization between *peninsulares* and criollos increased, finally leading to the outbreak of the First War for Independence.

Into this turmoil José Martí was born on January 28, 1853. Martí's father, don Mariano, the son of a poor rope-maker in Valencia, Spain, had come to Havana as a sergeant in the Spanish army, hoping to find a better life there for himself and his young wife doña Leonor, herself the child of a modest Spanish family.

Very early it became clear that the first child of their union (soon followed by seven sisters), young José, was a bright and serious boy; although his father had minimal interest in seeing José pursue his studies, the boy's godfather felt otherwise, and agreed to pay for his education at the Municipal School for Boys in Havana. Through the godfather, José came to the attention of the poet and intellectual Rafael María Mendive, and from 1866 on this fine and sensitive man became José's friend, mentor, and teacher, and undertook the expense of his continued education. It would be impossible to measure the extent of Mendive's influence on the budding mind of this adolescent boy; suffice it to say that Martí's first true introduction to politics took place at Mendive's home and in his school.

Martí as a young boy was ideally suited for involvement in the political and social movements developing then in his country; for he was a romantic child, given to writing verses and to serious and intense immersion in the world around him. Very early he felt horror at the inequities existing on the island, and a deep sense of compassion for those less fortunate than he, in particular the Cuban slaves. It is reported that on learning of Abraham Lincoln's assassination (Martí was then twelve) he wept and solemnly joined the mass mourning which took place in Havana and throughout Cuba.

At fifteen Martí had his first encounter with the despotic power of the Spanish Crown. In the general atmosphere of fear and vigilance, Mendive was arrested for allegedly attending a political rally at a local theater. Despite protests and proof to the contrary, he was jailed for this crime in Havana, and Martí, ignoring his own safety and reputation, faithfully visited his teacher in prison. Mendive and his family were shortly thereafter exiled to Spain, and the gap left by his absence caused Martí to question further the system which so arbitrarily expelled its finest minds.

It was a small step from his involvement in Mendive's arrest to the more direct confrontation he very soon had with the authorities. In October, 1869, there was a large military parade in Havana; marching in it were young boys and men, anxious to show publicly their loyalty to the ruling Spanish. One of these boys was a fellow student of Martí's, and his blatant act of support for the Crown outraged Martí and his classmates. Following the parade, Martí and his best friend wrote a letter to the boy involved, accusing him of betraying the cause of all true Cubans. The authorities found the note, and on October 21 the two were arrested and confined in the Havana city jail. Four and a half months later, on March 4, 1870, the two were tried by a court-martial. José's friend was given six months; José himself, insisting throughout the trial that he alone was responsible for the infamous letter, received the harsh sentence of six years.

Thus, just seventeen years old, Martí began a period of his life that was to leave permanent physical and spiritual scars. As prisoner number 113, Martí labored in the government stone quarries, Las Canteras de San Lázaro. Chained about the ankles, the young man, already somewhat delicate in health and stature, spent his days with the other prisoners hacking away at the hard rock, under the merciless tropical sun. It is difficult to say whether the back-breaking work, the choking lime dust, the glaring sun, and the brutal guards affected the body of this boy more than the suffering and pain of those around him affected his soul. We do know that the experience left him iron-strong in his resolve to spend his life working for the freedom of all Cubans.

Thanks to army friends of his father's, Martí spent only six months in the quarries, and was then transferred temporarily to a prison on the Isle of Pines. In January, 1871, still half blind from the work in the sun and suffering from a hernia which troubled him for the rest of his life, Martí was deported to Spain in an act of leniency on the part of the court-martial. Once in Spain, he threw himself into his studies, earning degrees in civil and canon law and in philosophy and humanities in less than four years. He was then twenty-one years old.

It was in Spain that Martí seriously launched his writing career. His work had first been published in 1869, when his play *Abdala* appeared in a short-lived Cuban magazine, *La Patria Libre* ("The Free Homeland"). In Spain, however, he pursued his vocation with energy and success. His article on political prisons in Cuba, a masterpiece of strong and compassionate writing, won him the respect of intellectuals far older than he. His writings, for the most part political in nature, were extraordinary in their clarity and insight; his tremendous gift for language and his ability to present complex ideas in pristine form soon brought him to public speaking, a talent which he used with spectacular success throughout his life.

During the first twenty years of Martí's life, things were becoming more and more agitated in Cuba. We have seen that a variety of personal encounters with the tyranny of the Spanish colonial administration deeply affected the young man and convinced him of his role in the future liberation of Cuba. In October, 1868, even before his arrest and imprisonment, an event occurred which, from a distance, gave him faith in the possibility of final victory over the Spanish. In Oriente Province, a wealthy lawyer and sugar planter named Carlos Manuel de Céspedes joined with thirty-seven other planters to proclaim the independence of Cuba from Spain in what has come to be known as El Grito de Yara (the cry or proclamation of Yara, a town near Céspedes's plantation). This proclamation,

José Martí, apostle
of Cuban independence.

also a declaration of war, shook the foundations of Spanish rule and sent shivers of fear through all loyal *peninsulares* and criollos. For one of the first things Céspedes and his fellow insurrectionists did was to free their slaves and join with them in an integrated army.

Of course the political situation in Cuba at that time was such that the Grito de Yara was no surprise. In the proclamation Céspedes enumerated those offenses which were the main causes of the uprising: despotic government, excessive taxes, the exclusion of Cubans from most civic occupations and activities, and the lack of personal freedom in political, religious, and social life. Slavery, too, was seen as an evil, but this first truly organized uprising was tentative on the issue: in the Grito the eventual and indemnified emancipation of the slaves was declared, but no immediate and widespread abolition was foreseen. Thus, both liberals and radicals were temporarily placated.

The Grito de Yara began what is now known as the Ten Years'

War (1868–1878) or the First War for Independence, during which the United States supported Spain against the Cuban patriots. Initially Céspedes was successful with his troops; at the peak of the war, the rebels or *mambisos* controlled almost half the island. They even established a provisional government which included Tomás Estrada Palma, later to become the first president of the Cuban republic. But Spain sent reinforcements from the mother country, and the dreaded Volunteers saw the war as a true testing ground for their own passionate loyalty to the Crown. The fighting soon turned into guerrilla warfare, centered about the Sierra Maestra in Oriente Province, later the central stage of the Cuban Revolution.

In the cities also the conflict spread, leading to spontaneous and bloody confrontations between the opposing sides. On November 27, 1871, a large group of medical students gathered in a Havana cemetery. Rumors fast reached the Volunteers that the students were desecrating the grave of a Volunteer hero (this was never established), and without further ado they descended on the meeting and dragged the students to the captain general's palace. Here a council of war was called, and on the following day, at four in the morning, eight students were shot and thirty others condemned to chain gangs for from four to six years.

The following year José Martí organized a huge demonstration in Madrid to commemorate the massacre of the medical students. The incident had shaken him greatly, especially since friends of his had been involved, though not killed. For several years thereafter, the incident in Havana became a rallying point for mass demonstrations in memoriam and in protest.

By the time Martí graduated from his university studies he was despondent because he was unable to participate directly in the struggle going on in Cuba. Since he had been exiled, he was unable to return to Cuba legally, especially during the period of war. In order to be closer to home he decided to go to Mexico where he spent almost two years. Here he continued writing and began working as a journalist, a profession which later served him well in New York. His play, *Amor con Amor se Paga* ("Love Is Repaid by Love"), was successfully presented in Mexico City, and he soon gained on his own continent the renown he had enjoyed in Spain.

Impatient at being so near but so far from home, in January, 1877, Martí landed in Havana under an assumed name—he used his second name, Julián, and his mother's maiden name, Pérez—and spent a month at home without being identified. But his precarious position made it virtually impossible for him to work, and he soon returned to Mexico and then went to Guatemala. There followed months of writing, teaching, and speaking. During this period he met Carmen Zayas Bazán, the daughter of a wealthy Cuban exile, whom he married on December 20, 1877. They lived in Mexico and Guatemala until the Ten Years' War ended in 1878. A general amnesty was then declared by Spain, and the young couple were finally able to return to and settle in Cuba.

The Ten Years' War, lost by the rebels, left a deep wound in Cuban society. Hundreds of thousands of lives had been lost— 50,000 Cuban, 208,000 Spanish; the cost in financial terms was also astronomical. The rebels were by and large unhappy with the compromise which had ended the war, the Pacto del Zanjón. This treaty promised certain political freedoms to Cubans which were already enjoyed in Puerto Rico; it also promised Cuban representation in the Cortes, the Spanish parliament, and the abolition of slavery in 1886. The amnesty and the new political freedoms were short-lived, however, and things returned to what they had been before.

Even though the Ten Years' War had been lost by the rebels, the defeat had taken a long time, and this in itself was an encouraging sign that the Spanish monolith was more vulnerable than Cubans had been led to believe. Furthermore, the war had served as the training ground for many rebel leaders, some of whom survived to fight in the second and final war for independence. Céspedes, ambushed by Spanish troops toward the end of the war, had committed suicide rather than be captured. While the loss of his leadership was keenly felt, he was easily replaced by a far greater man, another military and political leader who had come to prominence in the war.

Antonio Maceo y Grajales, called the Bronze Titan, born in 1848, was the son of a free black small dealer in agricultural products living in Santiago de Cuba. He had little formal education, and at sixteen went to work as a muleteer. On his journeys across the island, young Antonio saw firsthand the cruelty of slavery, and very early developed a deep interest in political affairs. Despite the lack of a formal education, Maceo was keen and perceptive and soon caught the attention of a Santiago lawyer who introduced him into a group of merchants and other friends who were involved in "subversive" political activities.

During these days of plotting the rebellion against Spain, the Masonic Lodge served as an ideal group in which to plan with impunity; Maceo joined the Lodge in Santiago in 1864 and soon became a part of the most secret revolutionary circles. His father and

Antonio Maceo,
the Bronze Titan.

ten brothers also joined in supporting the movement, and later all twelve men were to fight and die in the struggle for Cuban independence. Maceo's mother, Mariana, is called by historians the motive force behind this total family involvement in the revolutionary movement.

Maceo joined the *mambiso* forces in the Ten Years' War and soon became famous for his courage and leadership. He rose rapidly in the ranks, eventually becoming commander. It was Maceo, perhaps more than any other leader, who perfected the guerrilla tactics that were primarily responsible for the war's lasting so long; the Spanish army was on countless occasions completely taken in by the almost invisible forces whom Maceo led into ambushes and lightning attacks against the superior forces of the enemy.

When not actually in battle, Maceo spent every free moment furthering his education through voracious reading and discussions with learned comrades-at-arms. He also organized the noncombatant life of the rebels; using the abandoned *palenques* (buildings used by runaway slaves and Indians during the early days of the colony), Maceo established hospitals, workshops, and living areas for the men and their families. The food stores were operated by his mother and his wife.

With the signing of the Pacto del Zanjón, Maceo was reluctant to give up the fight, believing that the compromise was not worthy of all those who had died in the war. In May, 1878, he was persuaded to leave for Jamaica with his family. He did not, however, give up his revolutionary struggle, and was soon to be joined by José Martí in the second phase of the war.

When Martí and his young bride returned to Cuba, they found things little better than before. The high point of their stay was the birth of their son, José Martí Zayas Bazán, to whom Martí was later to dedicate one of his loveliest collections of poetry, *Ismaelillo*. Unable to keep out of the continuing political turmoil, much to his wife's dismay, Martí spoke and published whenever possible his ideas on the necessity for Cuban independence. In August, 1879, there was an uprising in Oriente, an attempt to continue the war for independence. This brief struggle was known as La Guerra Chiquita ("The Little War") and was led by General Máximo Gómez and two of Maceo's brothers. There were mass arrests of suspected rebels, and Martí was accused of conspiracy and once again deported to Spain.

This time, however, he realized the value of living near Cuba, even though in exile. Therefore, in January, 1880, he went to New York. Here he lived in a boardinghouse inhabited mainly by Latin Americans, and run by a vivacious and intelligent Cuban woman named Carmita Mantilla. By the time Martí left Cuba, his marriage was failing, for Carmen disapproved of his political involvements, and it was not surprising that he formed a lifelong friendship with Carmita Mantilla in New York. Despite his frequent attempts at reconciliation with Carmen—including several visits by her and their son to New York—he felt closer to Carmita, with whom he had his second child, María. (María, by the way, eventually had her own child, the movie star César Romero.)

During the fifteen years Martí spent in New York—with frequent trips to numerous countries in Latin America—he was involved in organizing for the final war for independence. He spoke at count- less meetings, many of them with the Cuban tobacco workers in Tampa and Key West, Florida; wrote pamphlets and essays; and raised money and other forms of support for the Cuban movement. To earn a living he wrote art criticism for the *New York Sun* and was correspondent for several Latin American newspapers. He also served as diplomatic representative for Argentina and Uruguay.

This intense young man, with a high forehead and penetrating eyes, was a poet in his deepest self. During his long years of exile he found time to write poetry, essays, articles, plays, and children's stories. As a poet, Martí is considered one of the major pre-Modernist writers of Latin America. His early verses are romantic in tone and form, but he soon developed the baroque and jewellike style so typical of the later Modernists. Among his most famous collections are *Ismaelillo, Versos libres,* and *Versos sencillos,* which include the now famous poem/song "Guantanamera."

Martí's essays on American life and customs are a delight to read, for it is always interesting to see how an outsider views one's own people. His children's stories appeared in the four issues of *La Edad de Oro* ("The Golden Age"), a magazine for Latin-American youngsters which he published in 1889; they are mostly of a regional and historical nature, and still hold up very well today.

But Martí's major spiritual, intellectual, and physical energies went into the struggle for independence. One of the issues in this struggle which had still not been cleared up was the question of slavery and the role of the Afro-Cuban population in the movement. As has been pointed out, even among those fighting for independence from Spain, there were some who favored the maintenance of slavery, and others who felt that blacks were somehow less human than whites. Martí was not one of these. On the contrary, one of the most frequent themes of his speeches and essays was the need to unite *all* Cubans, regardless of color or origin, in the struggle for independence. His position was not merely a tactical one; Martí, profound lover of humanity in all its colors, could not conceive of a social doctrine which would not encompass all men and all women.

The question of the role of the Afro-Cubans had become a serious issue during the Ten Years' War. As part of the Spanish attempt to discredit the rebellion, vicious rumors were circulated implying that Maceo was more interested in establishing a black republic than in gaining liberation for all Cubans. He was accused of favoring black soldiers above white ones, and of encouraging the former to take over from their white officers. As befitted a man of high integrity, Maceo ignored these slanderous rumors for as long as he could. Finally, recognizing that his silence was feeding the fires of slander, Maceo wrote to the provisional government in May, 1876, asking that his name be cleared. No statement was forthcoming, however; the leadership itself was still ambivalent on the race issue. The vicious whispering continued and in 1880 Maceo was stripped of his command by the revolutionary junta.

Martí, always passionate in his defense of individual worth and rights, recognized also what a disastrous effect Maceo's expulsion would have on the revolutionary movement. Joined by other Cuban patriots, he protested the action, which was later rescinded.

The slavery issue was still a central topic in Cuba, too. At the start of the Ten Years' War, Céspedes had freed his own slaves and had declared the *eventual* abolition of slavery in Cuba. Céspedes's reason for this rather conservative position was most likely his desire to keep the support of those wealthy planters who, like him, wanted less Spanish control of the Cuban economy, but who, unlike him, wanted slavery to continue. However, those fighting in the Ten Years' War were primarily free blacks, runaway slaves, and poor criollo peasants, none of whom supported slavery. Very early in the war, Céspedes was petitioned to change his stand on slavery, and he refused. Instead, he came up with a compromise by which the slaves of rebel planters would not fight without their masters' permission, but the slaves of enemy planters could escape freely and fight with the rebels. A year later Céspedes finally agreed to the policy of encouraging all slaves to rise up, and by the end of 1869 the rebel leadership was almost entirely abolitionist.

The Pact of Zanjón, ending the war, had also promised the eventual emancipation of Cuban slaves. In 1879, the victorious Spanish government in Cuba agreed to a modified abolition plan whereby all slaves would be freed in 1880, but would be required to serve a tutelage period known as the *patronato,* in order better to "prepare" for full freedom. This was done so as to avoid the necessity for indemnification, or paying the slave owners for each slave freed. Naturally, the *patronato* system was little better than slavery, and it very soon broke down. Since the slave owners had to continue feeding and clothing their "ex"-slaves for several years, during the slow season as well as the harvest, most found it more profitable to free their slaves outright and then hire them back at low wages only during the active seasons. In 1886 the *patronato* system ended, and finally slavery was officially abolished in Cuba.

The period between 1880 and 1895 saw little or no fighting on Cuban soil, but the revolutionary forces were nevertheless most active in planning the future campaign. Especially in New York,

Cuban patriots training in New York.

the exiled leadership planned, collected funds, gained the secret support of members of the United States government, and in general girded themselves for the final battle. Early in 1890 Martí and Rafael Serra, a black Cuban exile, organized La Liga ("The League"), a group which hoped to promote the education and advancement of Afro-Cuban exiles. Martí was active in setting up classes and lectures, finding space, and teaching a class every Thursday evening. The content of his lectures was basically political; once again he spoke with passion about the need for total independence for Cuba, and the absolute necessity for the new society to be based upon the needs of the poor people, black and white.

On January 5, 1892, Martí organized the Partido Revolucionario

Cubano ("Cuban Revolutionary party") in New York, and the movement for independence entered its final stages. After many meetings
with other exiled leaders, in Santo Domingo, Jamaica, and Costa
Rica, the plans for the invasion of Cuba were completed on December 25, 1894. Three ships had been fully equipped and the *Amadis*
sailed for Costa Rica where it was to pick up Maceo and his expedition. Although the plans suffered an initial setback, by February
24, 1895, the Second War for Independence had started, with uprisings all over Cuba. On April 11 of that year, José Martí landed
in Cuba and joined the battle. He was shortly proclaimed major-
general, and led his troops through the mountains of Baracoa to
meet Maceo and his men. On May 19, 1895, mounted on a white
horse and at some distance from his aides, Martí was recognized
by a Spanish soldier and killed, at the age of forty-two. Less than a
year later, Maceo, too, was killed in battle.

Although Martí did not live to see the triumph of the Cuban
forces for independence, there is no doubt that he felt confident of
their eventual victory. Only a few years later, in 1902 the Republic
of Cuba was born.

José Martí, personification of the revolutionary struggle, called
by many the Apostle of Freedom, took his place in the pantheon
of Cuban heroes, and has been hailed by groups and individuals of
all political shades and of all nations as the father of Cuban independence. A couple of movies have been made of his life; postage
stamps have been issued in Cuba in his memory—and Senator George
Smathers of Florida suggested in 1959 that a Martí stamp be issued
in the United States in the Champions of Liberty series. Cuba is
dotted with statues of Martí, and although its construction was
delayed, a statue is also displayed in New York's Central Park. Near
Jerusalem, in Israel, there is a José Martí Forest, planted by two
Cuban Zionists.

But public adulation aside, Martí contributed vastly to the growth
of the revolutionary movement and to its ultimate success. He gave
his life for it, while he lived and in his death. He was also one of
the first Cubans to recognize the dangers inherent in accepting too

much aid from the United States, for he understood the economic interests that motivated official North American support for the independence movement. Having lived in New York for so long, he feared, justifiably, that once Cuban independence was established, the United States would, in effect, attempt to take the place of the expelled Spanish rulers. Sadly, this is what in fact happened.

6

A Confusion of Victors and a Profusion of Spoils

> ". . . the United States may exercise the right to intervene for the preservation of Cuban independence . . ."
>
> *Platt Amendment, Article III*

During his last years, José Martí focused more and more of his writings on the dangers he sensed in the United States' growing interest in its island neighbor. While he felt great admiration and affection for the ordinary North Americans whom he had come to know during his years of exile in New York, Martí recognized perhaps more clearly than any of his compatriots that American economic interests would very soon shape American behavior toward Cuba. Shortly before he died, in a moment of pessimism and despair, Martí wrote of the United States: "I have lived in the monster and I know its entrails." Harsh words, perhaps, for the country which had taken him in as an exile and had provided arms and money to help him and all patriotic Cubans wage their struggle against Spanish dominion. Often, however, the truth is harsh, and in this case

Martí was right: the course of events following close upon his death left no doubt as to the nature of North American intentions.

During the final years of Cuba's war with Spain, although the revolutionaries were greatly outnumbered and suffered many defeats, it became increasingly clear that Cuba ultimately would free itself from the despotic mother country. Pressures on the government in Washington grew; American businessmen clamored for the maintenance of Spanish control in order to protect their investments in Cuba, and the proindependence factions urged United States involvement to bring an end to an intolerable situation of colonialism. And as the battle intensified in Cuba, and the Spanish army was reinforced by the thousands, stories of atrocities and massacres filtered into the United States and further outraged those who supported Cuba's fight for independence. When, in 1896, the Spanish Crown sent General Weyler (known as The Butcher) to govern the island, his exaggeratedly brutal policies finally swung the pendulum in favor of the rebels. For Weyler, fearing the growing support that the independence fighters were gaining among the peasants, hastily erected a number of concentration camps, or *reconcentrados,* and into these he herded, at random, men, women, and children so as to "protect" them from the rebels. Conditions in these camps were unspeakable, and before they were closed down, thousands of Cubans had perished there from disease and starvation.

Fearing the consequences of an all-out war which would reach the cities as well as the countryside, and might damage American property in Cuba, the American consul in Havana urgently requested that a U.S. Navy ship be dispatched to Cuba in the event that American lives and property were threatened. The U.S.S. *Maine* was sent, and the mysterious explosion which destroyed it twenty-three days later, killing 260 members of its crew, provided the United States with just the right opportunity for entering the war. In justified anger at the destruction of its ship and its men's lives (although it has never been fully established whether in fact the explosion was an act of Spanish sabotage, as charged) the United States government sent a strongly worded ultimatum to Madrid;

Spain agreed at the last minute to meet the terms of the ultimatum, but the U.S. Congress nevertheless declared war. The date was April 11, 1898.

Four months later Santiago de Cuba was captured and the war was over. The slogan of the American fighting men in Cuba was "Remember the *Maine!*"; it should not be forgotten that for the Cubans a great deal more than one ship and 260 lives was at stake, and had been for years, not months. The Cubans had been fighting

The Presidential Palace, Havana.

and dying since 1868, and it was they who had brought the war to the point where it took only four months to end it.

Now Martí's worst fears began to be confirmed, for the American forces in Cuba soon took over the whole enterprise and even deprived the Cubans of a true celebration of their hard-won victory. When the United States had declared war, it had publicly disclaimed "any disposition or intention to exercise sovereignty, jurisdiction or control over [the] island" and determined "to leave the government and control of the island to its people." How soon these honorable words were forgotten! An American general, seconded by American soldiers, accepted Spain's surrender in Santiago, while the Cuban soldiers and their officers were literally forbidden to enter the city, not even to attend the surrender ceremonies. American diplomats sat with Spain for the signing of the Treaty of Paris which laid down the terms of the victory, granting the territories of Puerto Rico, Guam, and the Philippines to the United States. American military personnel appointed the officials who would administer the newly liberated island, and all of their appointees were the same men who had loyally served Spain during the bitter years of struggle. Americans ordered all members of the Cuban revolutionary army disarmed, while U.S. soldiers patrolled the streets and the countryside of Cuba. The American army imprisoned or exiled Cubans who protested that this was not the kind of independence they had been seeking. And Americans ruled Cuba for three years by means of a military occupation force. No wonder it seemed to many Cubans that they had merely exchanged one master for another.

As plans for the establishment of a government developed, it became clear that here, too, the United States would accept nothing less than passive agreement to its own desires. The Cuban constituent assembly, though elected by the Cuban voters, did not in fact write the Cuban constitution; they were presented with a constitution which had been drafted in Washington, and were simply told to accept it. While there was some resistance, the document was eventually approved, and even the nefarious appendix, known as the

Platt Amendment, was accepted by the Cuban delegates, for fear that further resistance would lead to greater U.S. control.

The Platt Amendment was to form the basis for decades of anti-American feeling in Cuba. For this amendment, introduced in Washington by Senator Platt of Connecticut, not only gave the United States two naval bases on the island (Guantánamo Base near Santiago remains today as an American naval station), but also gave the United States a priori approval to intervene in Cuba's internal affairs if and when it saw fit, with or without the invitation of the Cubans.

Among the other institutions imposed by the United States on Cuba was its educational system. Modeled exactly on the system of public education in Massachusetts, the Cuban schools were in no way designed to meet the needs and fit in with the traditions of the Cuban people; their first teachers were even sent to Harvard University for training, and there they learned from American textbooks and were taught by American professors so they could return to educate Cubans.

This, then, was the situation immediately after Cuba won independence. While it may be difficult to understand why the United States felt itself justified in taking such a stand with regard to another sovereign nation, the issue is perhaps clarified when we note that even at the time when the United States declared war on Spain, in 1898, there were already over $50 million worth of American investments in Cuba, and by 1909 this had risen to $141 million. The end of the war saw the frantic purchasing of Spanish plantations and sugar refineries, as well as public utilities, by large American corporations. By 1903 Cuba was all but totally dependent economically on the United States: Cuba was exporting $34 million worth of goods to the United States annually, and $25 million worth of American goods entered Cuban ports. Only relations of a close and reciprocal nature would assure the continuance of the profits gained by American business through economic investments in and agreements with Cuba.

The power of the economic interests, and the Platt Amendment propping open Cuba's door, were all that was needed to guarantee the American moneyed community a free rein on the island. Add to this the series of weak governments following independence and the frequent interventions by United States Marines when opposition became too threatening, and you have several decades of virtually uninterrupted prosperity for the wealthy Cuban and American business community, and of grinding and deadening poverty for the mass of Cuban workers and peasants. Because the governments, although usually elected, functioned primarily for the benefit of those powerful moneyed interests, little of substance was done to improve the lives of the Cuban population, and the governments were riddled with dishonest and power-hungry men who were more interested in making personal fortunes than in governing their country democratically.

Cuban slum of the 1950s.

As the situation worsened for the majority, there was greater resistance both to the Cuban governments in power and to American presence on the island. And as resistance mounted, the incidence of ruthless repression increased. One president, José Miguel Gómez, was known as El Tiburón ("The Shark") because of the way he ruled the country. He instituted illegal racist policies disenfranchising the black and mulatto population, hardly half a century after the abolition of slavery. But while Gómez and others were corrupt and brutal, the prizes for pure despotism must surely go to Gerardo Machado and Fulgencio Batista.

Gerardo Machado was elected president of Cuba in 1924, and through a series of Machiavellian maneuvers managed to stay in the presidential palace until 1933. Among his achievements were the abolition of the vice-presidency, the suspension of constitutional guarantees, and the assassination of labor leaders, political critics, and students who opposed his regime. His henchmen, called *porristas,* were credited with the murders of thousands of people only vaguely suspected of antigovernment sentiments. He finally overstepped his bounds when, in 1929, he sent gunmen to Mexico to assassinate the exiled Cuban student leader Julio Antonio Mella, young, handsome, brilliant, and tremendously popular among Cuban intellectuals and workers alike.

Mella's murder led to a series of general strikes and to the development of superbly organized resistance movements, centered around the University of Havana. So threatened did the government feel, that in 1930 Machado ordered not only the university, but also all high schools and normal schools, closed indefinitely. Given the generalized political unrest and the great depression of the 1930s—which caused sugar prices to plummet and unemployment to leap to new heights—Machado began to lose his grip on the country. When the United States saw the full extent of Cuba's instability, it threw its support behind Machado's opposition and called upon the Cuban army to effect his overthrow. Machado was forced to flee to Nassau.

Fulgencio Batista was a young army sergeant who at first seemed to be concerned with the establishment of a truly Cuban democracy and the end of foreign intervention, so much so that when he and his fellow sergeants took over Camp Columbia in 1933 and had a new government appointed, the United States refused to recognize it for it was too liberal and anti-American. Soon, however, the American ambassador to Cuba, Sumner Welles, saw that Batista was the best horse to back, and between the two of them they came up with a presidential candidate, Colonel Carlos Mendieta. A perfect candidate, for he followed blindly the counsel of Batista. For almost twenty-five years, either behind the throne or on it (he served officially as president from 1940 to 1948, and again from 1952 to 1958), Batista ran the island in the best traditions of tyranny.

Batista's credits read much like Machado's, with the important difference that he enjoyed even greater American support, and this time not only moral but in the form of arms and money. And Batista had longer than Machado to play out his drama. Batista was responsible for the imprisonment or exile, the torture and execution of thousands of people. It is estimated that Batista caused the murders of over twenty thousand Cubans—men, women, and children—in the pursuit of a tranquil term of office without opposition. It is no wonder that when he ran for a second term in 1952 he was the only candidate.

The full horror of the Batista period cannot possibly be conveyed in print. Photographs and documents are available attesting to the grisly methods this man used to maintain his position of power. One example will suffice. Batista's lackeys, charged with the job of keeping public order at any price, developed the system of leaving the mutilated corpses of their male victims on the doorsteps of their homes. This way the man's family—mother and father, sisters and brothers, wife or girlfriend, children—would literally stumble upon the body in the morning and would perhaps learn that it was dangerous to protest against the government.

In the meantime, American business interests had never had it so good; Cuba's doors were opened even wider than before to welcome investors. By the late 1950s American businesses controlled 90 per-

Havana's Chief of Police Carratala, close associate of Fulgencio Batista.

cent of Cuban utilities, especially electricity and telephones, and 50 percent of the railroads. Cuban sugar was 40 percent American-owned. What this meant was that the astronomical profits from these industries and others were earned in Cuba and immediately siphoned back into the United States, while extremely low taxes were paid to the Cuban government and even lower wages to the Cuban workers.

Other benefits awaited wealthy American tourists and gangsters on the island. Havana had grown into a glamorous and glittering city, famous for its casinos—one in every hotel—where the American Mafia and the gambling syndicates added to their already vast financial empires. The enormous gleaming hotels, the palatial resorts and country clubs catered to the most exclusive clientele of wealthy

Cubans and Americans and the international diplomatic community. As long as you were not either black or poor, you could luxuriate in any number of swimming pools, tan yourself on any number of private beaches, and enjoy the languor of the tropics at any number of country estates. And for those with more private pleasures in mind there were the 270 brothels in Havana, furnished to a large extent with girls as young as fourteen, as well as over seven hundred bars staffed by beautiful and imaginative "hostesses." Ironically, the main street in the "red light" district was named Calle Virtudes, "Street of Virtues"!

A frequent sight in the 1950s: Cuban children watching the gaming tables.

For the poor the daily struggle to survive became even more desperate. While most were not directly involved in the antigovernment movement, and therefore were not often the victims of direct government brutality, they did not enjoy the leisure and luxury of the government's supporters. Trapped in a cycle of excruciating poverty, the Cuban peasant or worker was lucky to live past forty. Over one-fourth of the population was illiterate, since schooling was primarily for the middle and upper classes, and in any case all members of a poor family had to work in order that most of them might survive. Even with all members working, life was not easy for the average Cuban family, for in the cities most workers earned less than $75 a month, and in the countryside the wage was 25 cents a day. The average per capita income in 1956 was $336. And of course that was only for those who could find work; unemployment in the cities reached epidemic proportions during the 1950s and the sugar and tobacco crop cycles were such that most agricultural workers worked only four months of each year. This explains, perhaps, why only 11 percent of all Cubans living in the countryside during that period ever drank milk, only 4 percent ate beef, and 2 percent ate eggs. At the same time, wealthy residents of Havana in 1954 purchased more Cadillacs than were bought in any other city in the world.

It should be clear that such a situation could not be allowed to continue. Even in the United States, toward the end of Batista's regime, voices were being raised in protest against continued American support of this clearly tyrannical government. In March, 1958, New York congressional representative Adam Clayton Powell read into the Congressional Record a detailed and documented account of the horrors of Batista's regime and then produced a staggering list of small and large arms and ammunition shipped from the United States to Batista since 1956. He called for an end to American military support for the dictator and urged that a more appropriate stance be taken to restore democracy to the island.

And of course in Cuba there had been for many years an increasingly organized and dedicated revolutionary movement whose aim it was to overthrow Batista and restore Cuba to its people. The Cuban Revolution, or some reasonable facsimile thereof, was inevitable by 1956. All it needed was time to organize and the right people to lead it. For the Cubans had been fighting since 1868 to free themselves from foreign influence and corrupt governments, and after ninety years of waiting and dying, enough was simply enough.

It should not have come as any surprise to those familiar with the situation in Cuba when, in January, 1959, the Cuban Revolutionary Army marched into Havana and Batista and his henchmen fled to the Dominican Republic. For, as Thomas Jefferson had written so eloquently almost two hundred years before, "whenever any Form of Government becomes destructive . . . it is the Right of the People to alter or to abolish it."

7

A Battle Is Lost, but the War Is Won

Condemn me. It does not matter. History will absolve me.

Fidel Castro Ruz

The fall of the Batista regime was really initiated by Batista himself, with his coup d'etat on March 10, 1952. It seemed that this time the Cubans had finally had enough of corrupt, dishonest, and tyrannical governments, and the coup was followed by over a year of student uprisings and demonstrations, underground acts of sabotage, and the like. The government knew only one way to respond, and the brutality and violence for which Batista was already so infamous increased a hundredfold, and further pushed the Cubans to resist.

The first major blow against Batista was struck on July 26, 1953, when a group of 125 young men and two women launched an attack on the Moncada Barracks and other buildings of strategic importance in and around Santiago de Cuba. Although the plan failed, the Moncada attack had one essential element of importance: here for the first time the young lawyer Fidel Castro became directly involved in armed struggle, and it was during that bitter defeat that the nucleus of the guerrilla movement was formed.

Fidel Castro Ruz was born on August 13, 1926, on his father's sugar plantation in Oriente Province. Although he was born the illegitimate son of Angel Castro Argíz and Lina Ruz González, one of the house servants, the parents married soon after Fidel's birth. By Angel Castro's first marriage he had two children, and with Lina he had seven more, including Fidel.

A sturdy, stocky youth, full of energy and a great love of all physical activity, Fidel was educated in prestigious Jesuit schools in Santiago and Havana. It may have been through his own keen interest in learning that he in fact ever got to school, for his father, having had little formal schooling himself, saw no sense in his son's becoming educated. In any event, Fidel shone as a student, particularly in the humanities. His favorite subjects in primary school were agriculture, history, and Spanish. He also learned to play the bugle and excelled as an athlete. In high school Fidel became a superior basketball and baseball player and an excellent track runner. (Baseball is still one of Castro's favorite sports, and he always opens the season in Cuba.) When he graduated from high school in 1945 his yearbook said of him: "He was a true athlete, always defending the school colors with courage and pride. He has won the admiration and affection of all. He plans to make law his career and will no doubt fill the book of his life with pages of brilliance."

At the age of nineteen Fidel entered the University of Havana Law School. He was, by then, over six feet tall, in excellent physical condition, and already displaying those qualities of leadership and charisma which were to serve him so well in later life. In those days at the university black students were not allowed to play on the athletic teams, and Castro was instrumental in organizing a group to protest that policy. He soon was elected president of the student body and became even more involved in political activities, along with the majority of the university's students. Although to this day Castro claims to have been no more than a mediocre student, his final reports before graduation show him to have been superior academically in law, philosophy, and history.

While still at the university, Fidel married a philosophy student, Mirta Díaz Balart, on October 12, 1948. Mirta's family disapproved of the match, for by then the young law student was notorious in university circles, and was certainly not one to hide his already radical political beliefs from his in-laws. It would seem that neither family gave the young couple much financial assistance, because while on their honeymoon in Miami they ran out of money and the young groom was forced to pawn his watch and other items in order to buy their tickets home. On September 1, 1949, their son Fidelito was born. (Although the couple was divorced in 1955, and the boy lived for a while with his mother in the United States, he returned to Cuba just in time to join his father on his triumphant entry into Havana on January 8, 1959, and has lived there ever since.)

All of the qualities apparent in the young Castro are things that present-day observers have never failed to note: his energy, his will, his brilliant, analytical mind, his personal courage. He loves to talk and has the remarkable ability to synthesize what others say, to pull together the various and seemingly disparate threads of a discussion into a completely logical whole. Even his famous public speeches, often lasting five hours or more, are rarely boring or repetitive.

Fidel Castro, who began life as a ten-pound baby, and who was known in the neighborhood as an overactive toddler, to this day has kept his almost maddening energy, always outstaying and outdistancing his companions. He eats voraciously—although he also fasts from time to time—and today sports a slight paunch, but burns most of his fat away during his waking and working hours, eighteen to twenty daily. He sleeps little, and has no fixed home, having set up several pieds-à-terre throughout Havana and the rest of the island. He has a small country retreat on the Isle of Pines where he likes to go occasionally to hunt, fish, and skin dive. Among his other leisure time activities are baseball, motorboating, and dominoes, a game which he plays at times for hours on end. He has a dog,

Guardián, that he raised from a pup, and many newsmen and others seeking interviews have been able to see Guardián and his master racing, playfully knocking each other down, and rolling together on the lawn. Although reputed—by his enemies at least—to be a heavy drinker, Castro in fact does not drink except at official functions, and then he does not enjoy it. He is, however, a heavy smoker—it is rare to see him without a large Havana cigar gripped between his teeth.

Not much was known about the twenty-seven-year-old lawyer when he was arrested after attempting to capture the Moncada Barracks

Fidel Castro pitching.

in Santiago. From his own accounts of the incident, and from those of other participants, we now know that the plan had been in the works for over a year, its inception no doubt dating from the Batista coup in 1952. The men who attacked the barracks—all under thirty and inexperienced fighters—were dressed in army uniforms, a ruse which backfired, for the group which was to reinforce the initial attack could not distinguish friend from foe. The major setback, however, occurred when the supporting group got lost in the winding narrow streets of Santiago, a city with which most of them were unfamiliar. By the time they arrived at Moncada, the small vanguard —outnumbered fifteen to one—was in dire straits. Seeing the inevitable defeat, Fidel ordered his men to retreat, and some of them were able to escape into the mountains, only to be captured later. The attackers were mostly wounded and killed, and the survivors arrested on the spot.

As the police rounded up more and more real or suspected insurrectionists, the brutality with which they treated the prisoners became known in the city. There was a general outcry and finally Monsignor Pérez Serantes, the archbishop of Santiago, intervened and personally pleaded for an end to the mass tortures and midnight roadside murders. The authorities agreed not to kill the rebels, but rather to let them stand trial for their act, with the full protection of the law. With this guarantee many of the young people surrendered. But the government forces did not in fact keep their word. Almost all of the revolutionaries were horribly tortured in prison, many of them dying there, for despite the promises of reduced harshness, an order had come from Batista that there must be ten rebels killed for every fallen soldier, and this was scrupulously carried out by the army.

Fidel Castro managed to escape for a while, but was eventually captured. He was lucky enough to be caught by a lieutenant who had been his classmate at the university, and rather than send the notorious rebel to the army jail, his friend had him transported to the civilian prison where he knew the prisoner would not be too badly treated and certainly not killed.

The group was brought to trial in September, 1953, and for a while Castro served as one of the defense lawyers, a privilege allowed by the court even though he too was on trial. However, his brilliant arguments threatened to weaken the prosecution's case, and the army arranged for two doctors to sign a statement to the effect that Castro was too ill to appear further. Thus, despite incontrovertible proof that his health had never been better, Castro was not permitted into the courtroom again, and was tried separately and secretly on October 16, 1953.

His trial was held in the nurses' lounge of the Santiago City Hospital, in the presence of three judges, two public prosecutors, and six journalists who were forbidden to take notes. Also in the room and in the corridors were almost a hundred armed soldiers and officers. Castro provided his own defense, primarily because the lawyer who had volunteered to undertake that risky job had been allowed only ten minutes with the defendant to prepare the case, and that in the presence of a sergeant from Military Intelligence. In fact, the whole trial was a travesty, for even as his own attorney Castro was denied law books, documents, and even a copy of the indictment. He was kept seventy-two days in solitary confinement and incommunicado before the trial, and was denied the public hearing which was constitutionally guaranteed to all Cubans.

Needless to say, despite his eloquent defense he was convicted and sentenced to fifteen years in the penitentiary on the Isle of Pines. However, the speech which he made at the trial, and was then able to write down in prison, has come to us in the form of an important document entitled *History Will Absolve Me*. In that speech, in which he enumerated the irregularities of the trial, the brutal mistreatment of the prisoners, and the details of the abortive attack, he also set down what were to become some of the more essential programs of the future revolutionary government.

The first seven months on the Isle of Pines Castro spent in solitary, but after that he was able to organize a school for the other inmates where he taught history and philosophy. He himself studied English and read on many subjects, from ancient Greek and Chinese history to religion and politics. He continued also to organize politically from his cell, smuggling out messages and speeches, including the text of *History Will Absolve Me* which his friends quickly printed and distributed widely. After a year and a half Fidel and the others were granted amnesty, Batista having given in to pressure from the more liberal sectors of Cuban society. The conditions under which they were freed stipulated that they cease all political activities.

For two months Castro tried to lead a quiet, legal life, but found this impossible. So he and some companions exiled themselves to Mexico, where they solidified plans for the overthrow of Batista. It was in Mexico that Fidel Castro met Ernesto Guevara, the Argentine doctor who was to become another major figure in the Cuban Revolution, and an internationally recognized symbol—of evil for some, of high revolutionary virtue for others.

Ernesto Guevara de la Serna was born on June 14, 1928, in Rosario, Argentina. His father, Ernesto Guevara Lynch, was a civil engineer, although during his life he practiced many occupations, including the farming of *yerba mate,* the tealike national beverage of Argentina. Both Ernesto, senior, and Celia de la Serna, the mother, had great-grandparents who had migrated from California; the father's stock was Irish and the mother's Spanish.

The baby Ernesto was a sickly child, suffering his first asthma attack at the age of two. His parents, worried that his disease might weaken him irreparably, did everything they could to help him. When he was four the family (including four more children) moved to Altagracia where the altitude and climate were much better for the child. Ernesto's mother kept him home from school, for she feared that the long bus trip and the rigorous life of the regular students would be more than the child could take. However, the authorities eventually forced his parents to send him to the local public school, but not before his mother had taught him French and had given him a broad cultural foundation.

In school Ernesto soon proved to be an excellent and mature student, always befriending boys older than himself, and constantly astonishing his teachers and his friends' parents by the precocity of his interests. On one occasion, when he was thirteen, he was found in the study of a classmate's father, avidly reading a book by Sigmund Freud; he also liked, at an early age, to recite the poetry of Pablo Neruda and other Latin-American poets, and he read hungrily whatever French works he could lay his hands on: Jules Verne, Alexandre Dumas, and Charles Baudelaire.

Once he began going to school he developed other interests as well. In order to combat the weakness produced by his asthma, he threw himself intensely into sports, preferring rugby, soccer, and touch football. He was even good enough to make the second team in high school. He seemed, in fact, to be a normal, intelligent student, indulging like any other boy in pranks typical of school days. A friend recalls that Ernesto was frequently spanked by one particular teacher. In retaliation he came to school one day with a brick hidden in the seat of his pants, so that when inevitably he was called to the front of the room for punishment, the teacher hurt herself on the brick instead of hurting the incorrigible student!

The family's finances were never very stable, primarily because Ernesto's father was so prone to changing professions. Eventually they moved to Buenos Aires where job prospects were better. After graduating from high school, Ernesto entered the medical school of the University of Buenos Aires, much to the dismay of his father, who had hoped he would continue the family tradition by studying engineering. But medicine had always interested the young Guevara, no doubt because of the discomforts caused by his own malady.

Next to sports, Ernesto's greatest passion was travel. As soon as he was old enough to leave home on his own, he spent as much time as possible moving around his country and his continent. On one occasion he bought a motorized bicycle and rode across some of Argentina's more remote provinces; another time he signed up on a merchant marine ship and sailed around the Caribbean. Shortly before finishing medical school he and a friend bought a motorcycle and rode (eventually walked and hitchhiked) through several Latin-American countries, working at odd jobs when they ran out of money. They spent a good deal of time at a Peruvian leper colony, where they set up sports programs and other activities for the patients.

During these trips the young medical student developed a keen interest in tropical medicine, and the beginnings of a strong social and political sense. He was later to say that the opportunity to see the realities of Latin America forced him into an awareness of the "misery, hunger, disease, the inability to cure a child for lack of money, the brutalization which continual hunger and punishment provoke," and he started to see that "there was something just as important as being a famous scientist or making a substantial contribution to medical science: and that was to help these people."

Returning once more to Buenos Aires, and more eager than ever to finish his medical studies, Guevara raced through his final requirements, completing ten to twelve subjects in a little over six months. At the age of twenty-five, in March, 1953, he graduated as a doctor. He did not, however, set up a practice, for his travels had whetted his appetite for a more adventuresome and politically active life.

On his way to join a friend in Venezuela he met an exiled Argentine doctor who persuaded Guevara to join him on a trip to Guatemala. Here they participated in the local revolutionary struggle, until it was put down by the intervention of United States Marines. Nevertheless, this period was important. He met Hilda Gadea, an exiled Peruvian whom he later married; he came into close contact with Cubans who had fled to Guatemala after Moncada, and through them he became more deeply involved than ever in the revolutionary movement.

It was also in Guatemala that he got his nickname, Che. *Che* is an Argentine expression which means "Hey, man!" and like most Argentines, Guevara's speech was liberally sprinkled with the word. It is significant that for Ernesto himself the whole period in Guatemala, a period when his future as an active revolutionary finally came into focus, was summed up in the acquisition of that name: "For me 'Che' signifies that which is most important, most beloved

Ernesto (Che) Guevara,
holding his asthma vaporizer.

in my own life. How could I not like it? Everything that came before, my first and last names, are small things, personal and insignificant."

When the Guatemalan situation got too dangerous, Che sought asylum in the Argentine embassy, and rather than return home he chose to go to Mexico. There he spent some months working as a street photographer, a risky job since he had no work permit. Eventually he was able to work in some capacity in the allergy ward of the Mexico City Hospital, and it was reportedly there that he first met the people who introduced him to Fidel Castro. In any case, it is known that when he met the young Cuban revolutionary they talked together into the early hours of the morning, and Che decided on the spot to join Fidel and the others in their plans to go to Cuba. This was in 1955.

The underground group of Cuban exiles in Mexico worked under great duress, being sought simultaneously by the Mexican police, the United States FBI, and Batista's secret agents. Nevertheless, they were able to rent several apartments and houses in the country, where they began storing arms and materiel and training men for the landing. During this period Che won the respect and admiration of his fellow revolutionaries, for his intelligence and his unshakable conviction that what they were doing was correct and that they would eventually triumph. He was a warm and humorous person, according to all accounts, but absolutely dedicated to what he was doing and extremely demanding of himself and of others. He had courage which often bordered on rashness, but was also imbued with compassion for the failings and weaknesses of others. Throughout his campaign journals he displays modesty toward his own accomplishments and generosity toward others.

Guevara's qualities and talents joined with those of Castro made for an unbeatable team, as history was soon to prove. Through months of careful and intelligent planning—collecting funds in Cuba, Latin America, and the United States; recruiting and training guerrilla fighters; maintaining secret contacts with underground groups on the island—these two men, and the many others who worked with them, were able to forge a group of loyal and dedicated followers in Mexico, and a backup group of dozens of men and women in Cuba. They purchased, for twelve thousand dollars, the fifty-eight-foot yacht *Granma,* and on November 25, 1956, left the Mexican port of Tuxpan for Cuba. None too soon, for the very next day the Mexican police raided most of their hideouts.

Of the men who sailed on the *Granma*—a stormy seven-day voyage, with eighty-two seasick and frightened men crowded into space for eight passengers plus crew—only twelve survived to go on and fight in the revolution. After landing at Playa de las Coloradas, they were rapidly dispersed and decimated by the Batista air force, ten of them were captured, and the rest wandered for days through the swamps. The twelve finally met on the Sierra Maestra in Oriente Province. They had only seven weapons, no ammunition, few supplies—most of them had survived on sugar cane, sap from vines, and, on one occasion, on the few drops of water which Che was able to extract from a rock with his asthma vaporizer.

The Sierra Maestra was an ideal area in which to recoup their strength and regroup their forces. The rugged terrain, well shielded by heavy foliage, had been the seat of Cuban revolutionary activities as far back as the Indian and slave uprisings, and more recently during the wars for independence. And the peasants in the sierra, mistrustful at first, were soon convinced that the guerrillas' fight was their fight. Many of them helped the men by bringing them food and supplies, and sheltering them in their *bohíos.* Eventually dozens, then hundreds, and finally thousands of peasants joined the

The yacht *Granma,* used by Fidel Castro and his men for the landing in Cuba.

rebel forces, serving not only as guides and couriers, but also as some of the most courageous fighters.

In exchange for their help, the rebel forces worked with the peasants on their farm chores, always paid them for food and supplies, and provided medical help to the sick. Furthermore, unlike soldiers in Batista's army, rebel soldiers guilty of pillaging were severely punished, and in the Rebel Army the penalty for rape was death. As the revolution progressed and larger territories fell under the guerrillas' control, small factories, clinics, stores, and workshops were set up for the peasants; rudimentary schools were established for the troops, many of whom were illiterate, and peasants attended classes also. Even the revolution's critics have usually had to admit that the rebels behaved with kindness, respect, and humanity toward the peasants.

Thus, what began with twelve tired and demoralized men in the middle of the Sierra Maestra ended in 1959 when an army of peasants, workers, students, professionals—men and women, Cubans from all walks of life—somehow managed to defeat Batista's army, his air force, his navy, and his police, a total force of over thirty thousand men armed with the most modern and efficient weapons. Throughout the revolution the men and women in the mountains used only those arms which they could purchase illegally in the cities or abroad, or those which they captured. Later they were often able to buy weapons from the government troops who were beginning to sense which way the wind was blowing. On one occasion, near the end of the revolution, a rebel column captured an entire army transport train carrying arms and materiel to the battlefield. Since for the major part of the revolution the Batista army had been provided with United States weapons—a policy which was only belatedly and reluctantly voted out by the United States Congress in 1958—many of the rebel victories were won with captured American arms.

While the rebels were ambushing the army in the mountains, and taking large and small army posts, the city forces were gathering strength for similar actions. On March 15, 1957, the Catholic leader José Antonio Echevarría led an attack by students on the Presidential

Palace in Havana, in an abortive attempt to assassinate Batista. During the summer of the same year angered electrical workers cut the cables that brought power to the capital, and for three days Havana was without electricity. As the situation grew hotter, large buildings and factories were bombed, and radio programs were constantly interrupted by invading revolutionary students. In general the city activities grew in proportion to the victories of the rebels in the countryside.

For much of this period Batista insisted to the world at large that nothing serious was happening in Cuba. He denied the presence of Fidel in the sierra, at times spread rumors of the death or capture of the guerrilla leader, and in general fiddled while Cuba burned. The myth that there were no guerrilla forces in the mountains was definitely and eloquently shattered by an article in *The New York Times* in February, 1957, written by Herbert L. Matthews. He had gone to the sierra to interview the controversial rebel leader and to prove his existence to the public. Despite claims by Batista, his supporters, and even some American politicians that what Matthews reported was untrue, the word was out and Latin America and Washington watched anxiously to see what would be the outcome of the revolution going on in Cuba.

As pressure on the Batista government increased, it in turn stepped up its brutal measures indiscriminately. By 1958 even the most respectable and nonrevolutionary groups and individuals in Cuba were clamoring for a halt to government repression. The Lions, the Rotary Club, the Masons, and professional groups of doctors, lawyers, dentists, architects, and professors publicly stated their disaffection with their government's actions. The Catholic hierarchy of the island, led by Cardinal Manuel Artega, called on Batista to abdicate and allow for the formation of a more representative and humane government. Respectable middle-class matrons throughout the island held masses for peace, and demonstrated in the city streets to protest the arrests and murders of their sons and daughters. Many of these protests were met with greater violence by the government, which on one occasion sanctioned the clubbing and hosing of a gathering of women in Santiago.

The official government stance continued to be that things were under control. Life seemed to go on as usual: the American elite came and went, enjoying the Cuban beaches and golf courses; tourists still flocked to the roulette wheels and gaming tables of Havana's plush casinos; movie stars came to make films in the island's beautiful tropical setting; Batista even called for elections on November 3, 1958 (only two months before he fled the country); and an American senator from Louisiana visiting Havana was quoted as saying: "Is there a revolution here? I hadn't noticed any trouble."

But despite all attempts to hide and distort the facts, the revolutionary forces won. What might have seemed to some a ragtag and

The Rebel Army enters Havana, January, 1959.

motley crew, whose leaders had little or no previous military experience—for the leadership included women from middle-class homes, a chauffeur, a stonemason, a printer, an engineering student, a salesman, a lawyer, a doctor, and several peasants—in fact gained so much popular support that it was able to defeat the army and take power.

On January 1, 1959, in the middle of the night, Fulgencio Batista and some of his closest associates fled by air to the Dominican Republic. On January 8, the victorious forces of the Rebel Army marched into Havana, while other units entered the other major Cuban cities. Everywhere they were greeted with enthusiasm and celebration; the Cubans were by and large overjoyed to be finally freed from the years of suffering and misery which the governments of Batista and his puppets had brought them. Most Cubans had little doubt then that what had happened was right and just, and the country then moved seriously on to the task of setting up the new society.

8

Invasions and Missiles, Prisoners and Exiles

The United States is operating against an enemy that it does not see, does not know, and does not understand.

Herbert L. Matthews

The world in general, and the United States in particular, was watching the events in Cuba during the late 1950s with interest and concern. Latin America was notorious for the frequency of its revolts, coups d'etat, and uprisings, but there seemed to be something quite different about the revolution taking place in Cuba. In the United States the press coverage of the two years of fighting was spotty and mostly inaccurate—with a few exceptions—and the American public had only the vaguest idea of the realities of the situation. Quite early along, certain groups and individuals were already trying to discredit the rebels in the sierra; once the fighting period of the revolution ended and the new government took over, these voices became louder, and at the same time international political tensions increased greatly.

One of the first acts of the new Cuban government was to close down most casinos and to lower all rents on the island by 50 percent. This directly touched many American businessmen who owned the enterprises and the buildings, and naturally caused ill will. Hundreds of Cuban refugees poured into the United States in the weeks immediately following the end of the revolution. Among these first exiles were many people who had been either directly involved in the Batista regime—officials, Armed Forces personnel, police—or who had been active in the more corrupt aspects of Cuban life—prostitution, gambling, abortion racket, drug traffic. Once in the United States these people, and the more respectable exiles who joined them, formed into underground groups (the best known was called Alpha-66) based primarily in Miami, Florida, and began making plans for an invasion of Cuba in order to overthrow the Castro government. In the first year and a half there were at least six incidents involving planes piloted by exiles that bombed Cuban cane fields and population centers. While these acts were committed without American sanction, the weapons and the planes were American-made, and the Cuban government was none too happy about this.

In other words, relations between the United States and Cuba were shaky from the outset. Despite the official American position of waiting to see how things developed, it was clear that powerful sectors of the United States government were already opposed to the Castro regime and were eager to see it toppled. These sentiments were helped along when, in 1960, Cuba resumed relations with the Soviet Union and signed the first Cuban-Chinese treaty in history. During the same year, and much to the anger of American business interests, thirty-six sugar mills and refineries were nationalized, as was the telephone company. All these enterprises had been American-owned. A little later during that year, over three hundred other companies and banks were taken over by the Cuban government, most of them also of United States ownership. By October, 1960, the United States had declared a partial embargo on trade with Cuba, limiting exports to a small number of basic necessities.

At the same time, Cuba had signed a treaty with the Soviet Union to trade sugar for oil. Although Cuba has never been rich in petroleum, several major American oil companies (Esso, Sinclair, and Texaco in particular) had large refineries on the island. When the first shipments of Russian oil arrived, the American refineries refused to process it. Cuba's response was immediately to nationalize the refineries, whereupon the United States withdrew all its technicians. Unofficially the Mexican government stepped in and some of its top petroleum experts went to Cuba to refine the Russian oil. This was what finally prompted the United States to stop buying Cuban sugar, to cut all exports from the United States, and, on January 30, 1961, to break diplomatic relations with the island's government.

The first major confrontation between Cuba and the United States is known both as the Bay of Pigs invasion and as the invasion of Playa Girón. Its secret name was Operation Pluto. Presumably organized and led by the "Cuban Revolutionary Council" in Miami, the plan was to train fifteen hundred men, arm them, supply them with ships and tanks, and lead them on an invasion of Cuba. They were to be greeted enthusiastically by the Cuban people who, according to American CIA information, were only too anxious to rid themselves of Castro. The invasion was announced, so to speak, by the bombing, on April 15, 1961, of two Cuban airfields. B-52s with Cuban markings flew over the island, hoping to create the illusion that this was the start of an uprising among the Cuban military. In fact, it was soon established that the planes were American-made, had been painted with the Cuban insignia by the CIA, and had been flown from Nicaragua by Cuban exile pilots. The bombings killed seven people and wounded forty-four; at the same time, the rumor of a landing in Oriente by exile groups and United States Marines was spread in order to divert Cuban forces from the real point of the landing, Playa Girón on the southern coast.

The Cuban government responded immediately by rounding up and jailing all known counterrevolutionaries and all those even remotely suspected of hostility to the regime. The thousands arrested included bishops and other clergy, many journalists—especially foreign—and the real underground (the largest group of those arrested), including twenty-five hundred CIA agents. Naturally, this took out of action all those who might have responded favorably to the invasion, and was an immediate blow to its success.

Meanwhile, at the United Nations in New York, Raúl Roa, the Cuban foreign minister, charged the United States with aggression against Cuba, a sovereign nation. The United States delegate, Adlai Stevenson, denied these charges and publicly vowed that there had been no American participation in the invasion. He even claimed that the planes used were Cuban, a detail which was soon contradicted when several were shot down over Cuba and were clearly marked "Made in U.S.A." During the same United Nations meetings the Guatemalan delegate denied all charges that his country had provided training facilities for the exile groups, another "fact" found to be untrue: the then dictator of Guatemala, Ydígoras, later revealed that he had provided such facilities for the expedition on the promise of cash from the United States and a more favorable trade policy between the two countries. (The cash was apparently never forthcoming.) The deceit extended so far that the invaders themselves were told by their CIA trainers that the bombing mission had been totally successful, destroying almost all of Castro's air force.

On April 16, President John F. Kennedy secretly authorized the expedition to continue and land on the beaches. It was also on this date that for the first time Castro declared the Cuban government to be socialist in nature. It must be remembered that until this date, two and a half years after the revolution, the term *socialist* had not been used by the Cubans themselves.

On the evening of April 16, the fleet of exiles—comprising fifteen hundred men, two United States battleships, and three freighters loaded with United States tanks and artillery and escorted by two Navy destroyers—joined American landing craft several miles south of Cuba. The men in the expedition were mostly middle- and upper-class exiles, with some workers, and of the fifteen hundred, fifty were black or mulatto. Over a hundred of them had been soldiers in Batista's army, and there were also three Spanish priests who had previously lived in Cuba. Many of these men were known by both the Castro regime and by the exile leadership as having been among Batista's most notorious and efficient killers. The brigade included not only former Batista soldiers and police, but also the ex-owners of more than eight hundred thousand acres of land in Cuba, close to ten thousand buildings and houses, and business enterprises including factories, cabarets, sugar mills, mines, banks, and newspapers. In other words, that group represented a great deal of lost wealth.

On the morning of April 17, the landings started. Despite the fact that President Kennedy had specifically ordered that no American was to participate in the landing, the first two frogmen to walk onto the Cuban beach were American citizens, working for the CIA.

While even Castro admitted later that the landing site had been well picked—the Bay of Pigs is a long and narrow bay on the southern central coast in a relatively inaccessible spot, surrounded by land and swamp which lend themselves to guerrilla fighting—the plan was poorly conceived and poorly carried out. Furthermore, the expected response of the Cuban people was not forthcoming; on the contrary, the people mobilized firmly behind the Castro government. Thus, although the invaders, helped by paratroopers who had been dropped inland, were able briefly to hold two small villages, and although their lost supplies were partially replaced by air drops from American B-54s, within forty-eight hours the invasion was defeated and the invaders captured. At 5:30 P.M. on April 19, 1961, the Bay of Pigs fell to the Cuban government forces and the invasion was over, a miserable failure for the exiles and a tremendous embarrassment to the United States government.

Of the 1,500 invaders, the Cuban forces captured 1,180, including most of the leadership. About 120 had been killed during the confrontation. No one, not even the major leadership, was executed after the capture: all the prisoners were tried and sentenced to long terms in prison. After one and a half years the leaders were ransomed for $175,000 and the remaining men were exchanged for $53 million worth of medical and food supplies. These arrangements were made between the Cuban government and private groups and individuals in the United States. A fact which has received virtually no attention in the United States is that Castro released the prisoners before receiving all the supplies; he let them go in time to reach home by Christmas, 1962.

It is relevant at this juncture to examine the whole question of prisoners and prisons in Cuba, for it is an area which has often been discussed and more often been distorted.

In the months immediately following the revolution up to twenty-five hundred prisoners were taken and tried, and seven hundred were sentenced to death. Those who were executed were responsible for the most heinous crimes encouraged by the Batista regime; lesser offenders were sentenced to prison terms of varying lengths. During that period local and foreign observers noted that the Cubans did not give in to their very human desire for revenge, but rather left the meting out of punishment to the military tribunals. A Cuban professor wrote to his brother in New York at the time, praising the moderation of the population: "It is marvelous to see the civic spirit and equanimity which the Cubans have shown at all times, the civilian as well as the military, especially after the horrors and monstrosities committed by the Batista regime have become known . . . it is marvelous, I say, to see that the people have not lynched these men. . . . No one is condemned without a conclusive trial."

Today the bulk of the political prisoners (about ten thousand) are people who to one degree or another have been caught at or suspected of counterrevolutionary acts, and by now many American and other foreign journalists have had the opportunity to visit the prisons, take photographs, and speak freely with the inmates.

In early 1963 a widespread rehabilitation program for political prisoners (many of whom are peasants) was established throughout the island, under the aegis of the Ministry of the Interior. It has been judged by observers to be one of the most effective and innovative programs of its kind anywhere. The aim of the program is to educate the political prisoners generally and politically and to train them for a profession or an occupation, so that when they are re-

Playground in a day care center.

leased they will be productive members of society and will not return to their antigovernment activities.

The special program called "Plan Two" is a representative one to examine. This particular plan encompasses the rehabilitation not only of the prisoners but also of their families, all of them peasants. The wives and families are moved to Havana, into mansions in the Miramar section, which used to be the wealthiest residential area and now houses not only the prisoners' families but also hundreds of thousands of scholarship students. The families are given free housing, clothing, food, education, day care centers, and general social services by the government. While the men in the prison farms receive general education—beginning with basic literacy if necessary—and training in agricultural or construction work (those who have a skill are encouraged to improve it), their wives also receive basic education and training for jobs, and their children go to schools in Havana, along with other schoolchildren. The women's programs are sponsored and carried out by representatives of the Federation of Cuban Women, and include hygiene and personal care, cooking, sewing, literacy, and general elementary school subjects. Once or twice a week, like the prisoners in the various rehabilitation programs, they receive informal political instruction. Neither the prisoners nor their wives are expected to become involved and active revolutionaries; it is simply hoped that their negative feelings about the government will be changed for more constructive ones.

The men, meanwhile, live in barracks on the prison farms, working and studying there. Once every forty-five days they spend three days with their families in Miramar (prisoners in other plans go home for visits also). They are given round-trip fares and money for food and are sent off alone; they need not report to anyone on arrival, and are simply expected to be back at the prison on time.

A prisoner in any program, including Plan Two, is eligible for release after having served a minimum of 25 percent of his sentence and after having been in some rehabilitation program for at least a year. In addition, the conduct, work record, and general progress of the prisoner (and his family, if in Plan Two) are evaluated. Prisoners in other plans then return home, where they are given jobs and counseling. They do not report to anything like a parole board— from the day of their release they are on their own.

The prisoners and families in Plan Two are sent to a new town called Sandino City, built especially for these families. Here they are given a house with two to four bedrooms, fully supplied with furniture, linens, dishes and silverware, utensils, and a ten-day supply of food. Men work on nearby farms or in town, and women, if they are able to work, are also given jobs in the city. By now, Sandino City is inhabited not only by ex-prisoners but also by other citizens.

While the failure of the Bay of Pigs invasion was a tremendous victory for Castro's Cuba, proving that it would take more than a mere landing to bring the government down, and that Castro had a great deal more support from the people than had been hoped, it also alerted Cuba to the possibility of further attacks. It became evident that exile groups would try again to invade, that an underground network on the island would be encouraged, and that the United States was even more openly hostile than had been thought. For these reasons, when the question of placing Soviet missiles on the island arose, the Cuban government agreed.

Subsequently, United States U-2 reconnaissance planes photographed what looked like a missile site on the island, and the markings on the weapons were clearly Soviet. On October 16, 1962, President Kennedy was first informed about these missiles, but the American public did not know about them until five days later. In the interim high-level secret talks were held among governmental officials to determine the best stance for the government to assume in response to what was felt to be a blatant challenge by the Soviet Union. We have learned since that at most times several members of the American government were holding out for air strikes and land attacks against Cuba in order to destroy the missiles and expel the Castro government. At all times, however, President Kennedy, his brother Robert (then attorney general), Robert McNamara, and a few others felt that such a step would be too threatening to world peace.

Premier Khrushchev of the Soviet Union was of course immediately contacted. In his response, he offered to remove the missiles if the United States would guarantee that it would not participate in another attack on Cuba. During this time, the United States had set up a complete quarantine or blockade around Cuba, preventing any foreign ships from reaching the island.

For seven days the world waited, closer perhaps to World War III than it had ever been. Since most of the negotiations were top secret, there was no way for the average citizen to know in what direction things were going. While there was no panic in the U.S. or in Cuba, tensions were high in both countries. The United Nations was called into emergency session to see what it could do to help; the Organization of American States (OAS) met and by unanimous vote (since Cuba had already been expelled from the organization) supported Kennedy's actions; heads of state from around the world offered advice and support to Cuba, to Russia, or to the United States.

The final outcome was a letter from President Kennedy agreeing to Khrushchev's terms, much against the advice of the Joint Chiefs of Staff, and on October 27 the Russians agreed to remove the missiles. A month later the United States called off the military blockade of Cuba.

The years since the missile crisis have been relatively quiet ones in Cuban–United States relations, although there have been attempted landings by exiles based in Florida, arrests of Cuban fishermen by American coast guards, and incidents of violence and sabotage on the island. Cuba's relations with the Soviet Union have been smooth also, with Russian aid and technicians coming to Cuba as part of the economic and trade agreements signed by the two countries. Cuba and China have been on reasonably good terms as well. However, in the case of both Russia and China, there have been indications of some serious differences with Cuba on several occasions which have been reflected in public statements by Castro or by other members of the government, rather than in specific actions or programs.

Just as some nations have criticized Cuba and have taken positions hostile to the Castro regime, so hundreds of thousands of Cuban citizens have, for various reasons, left the island. The earliest of these exiles, like those who participated in the Bay of Pigs invasion, were primarily well-to-do people. They were soon followed, in the two or so years after January 1, 1959, by large groups of professionals: doctors, lawyers, dentists, architects, professors and teachers, engineers and technicians, ministers and priests. In early 1961 some white- and blue-collar workers began emigrating. A small minority of these people were black; fewer than half of all the exiles had played any role in opposing Batista.

The exiles have left Cuba in various ways. Before commercial flights between Cuba and the United States were suspended, many left by that route. After the break in relations between the two governments, exiles went to other countries—especially Spain and Mexico—and from there to the United States. There was a period when Castro opened up the fishing port of Camarioca to any boat from the U.S. which came to get family members or friends. There were also hundreds of American airlifts from Cuba to Florida between 1965 and 1970. In 1971 the total number of exiles in the continental United States was 625,000, in Puerto Rico close to 30,000, in Spain 24,000, and in Latin America 49,000. That means that by 1971 there was a total of about 730,000 exiles in all.

They emigrated for a variety of reasons, as several studies have shown. The very wealthy left because they had lost their wealth, the counterrevolutionary because they feared imprisonment in Cuba, the religious because they feared atheism would take over, the racist because they feared black Cubans would take over. Most of them left either because they were joining members of their families who had left Cuba earlier, or because they were frightened by socialism. Rumors circulated that Castro would forcibly take all children away from their families, forcibly draft young men and women into the army, forcibly confiscate all personal property. These tales have been seen to be untrue. The Cuban government has in fact moved to strengthen the nuclear family; the army has a draft, like many armies, but does not conscript women; the only private property which has been confiscated is large, profit-making property such as industries, real estate, massive land holdings, but not personal belongings like cars, housing, clothes, books, and so forth.

Most of the Cuban exiles in the United States are concentrated in Miami, Florida, where one-quarter of the population is now Cuban. By 1970 over 30 percent of the business and financial interests in Miami were Cuban-owned, bringing in a total income of over $600 million a year. New York State, New Jersey, California, and Illinois also have large Cuban populations. The exiles have by and large been well treated in the United States, from a financial point of view. Employable male heads of households, for example, if they are Cuban exiles, receive one hundred dollars a month from the Welfare Department, although the same benefit is not extended to American citizens—welfare regulations forbid the granting of money to the unemployed male head of a household unless he is physically or mentally unable to work. Many government and private agencies have been working to help the exiles get jobs, training, licenses, and citizenship—for ex-Cubans it has been infinitely easier to achieve all these things than for the citizens of any other nation who seek to reside, work, or study in the United States.

Not everything has been so bright for the Cuban exiles, however. The darker-skinned Cubans have encountered prejudice from some white Americans, and many of them have also had difficulty getting jobs because of language and citizenship requirements. The biggest problem has arisen among the young people, the children of the exiles. They have been exposed to a totally new and different culture, and as a result there is a sharply growing generation gap and a serious delinquency problem. For example, in Dade County (where Miami is) the high school dropout rate is highest among Cuban youth, and there is increasing alarm at the high incidence of drug addiction and prostitution among Cuban juveniles.

So serious are the family problems faced by many Cubans in this country that in 1970 a well-known Cuban exile journalist wrote a bitter and impassioned article in the New York Spanish-language paper *El Tiempo,* in which he sharply criticized the policy of encouraging exiles to come to the United States. He wrote: "Those who took their children away from Cuba because they feared the government was going to take them away, now have neither children nor country. Those who feared the draft under Castro now see their children marched off to Vietnam. . . . Those who feared their children would be corrupted in Castro's Cuba now see them on the streets of Miami, New York, and Chicago participating in a process of social decay to which they are alien. They have broken all moral, economic, cultural, spiritual, and linguistic ties with their parents." Referring to the ever-present appeal of greater material wealth in the United States, Luis Ortega ends by saying: "A color TV set is not compensation for the loss of one's country and children," and urges that there be no more exiles.

In fact, Ortega is speaking for many who have come to feel that their flight from Cuba was perhaps precipitous. They have heard from relatives that things are not as bad as they had feared, that in fact in many ways things are a great deal better in Cuba than they had thought. Many Cuban exiles are now hoping for normalization of United States–Cuban relations so that perhaps one day they will at least be able to visit their homeland and families and see for themselves what is happening in Cuba.

9

Mobilization for Change

The country that bases its subsistence on one product alone commits suicide.

José Marti

What was it that made this small island so controversial once its government changed in 1959? What were they doing there, and what are they doing now, that provoked such strong reactions of anger or praise among people and governments from around the world? Although, as we have seen, hundreds of thousands of Cubans have left their homes and settled in a foreign country, why have the 8.5 million present inhabitants of Cuba chosen to remain there, and what are some of the aspects of their lives that have been touched by the revolution?

Even before Fidel Castro announced to the world that Cuba was a socialist country, there were fears in the United States that Cuba would "go over to the Communists." This was in fact the fear that Cuba would establish close ties with the socialist countries of Eastern Europe and with China, would confiscate American property on the island, and would thereby destroy the long-standing economic relations with the United States. For others this position expressed the concern that the people of Cuba would become less free under some kind of socialist government.

Before examining specific programs undertaken by the Cuban government since 1959, it is essential to understand clearly what exactly is meant by socialism, for a misunderstanding of this fundamental theory makes it impossible to comprehend the Cuban experience. Karl Marx, considered the father of socialism, believed and tried to prove that the real foundation of a society is economic. On this foundation rise the multiple superstructures of the society: its institutions, its political entities, its culture, and its social configurations. On the basis of this assumption, the socialist will maintain that while the importance of the superstructures is undeniable, they are at the same time significantly shaped by the economic structure underlying them.

Socialism in practice is based primarily on the abolition of the private ownership of the means of production: the factories, the large landholdings, the corporations which bring huge profits to the individuals or groups of individuals who own them. Under socialism the government or state owns and controls all industries, factories, stores, and services, and plans overall production so that it can most efficiently answer the needs of the people and the society. When the emphasis on personal profit is removed, and men and women are working at jobs which more directly benefit them and their fellow citizens, more humane working and living conditions should exist.

An essential aspect of socialist thinking is that there are certain services which are rights and not privileges, services which guarantee good health, housing, and food to all citizens. Thus, in order for the government to be able to provide these services to everyone, regardless of their individual power or skill, it is necessary for the whole economy of the socialist state to be carefully planned. Planning means a rational approach to what the people need, how much of it they need, how much of it the country is able to produce, how much will have to be imported, what the most efficient way is to produce all that is needed for internal consumption and external commerce, and what the most sensible means is to distribute essential goods and provide adequate services to the people. Since, in a socialist economy, individuals or corporations do not receive the profits, but the government instead redistributes what would have been profits, the government, with careful planning, is able to pay for and support the multiple services and benefits provided the population.

It is important to note that, while the term *communism* is freely used in the Western world to classify those countries with a socialist economy, this is an inaccurate designation. According to Marxist theory, communism has not been reached by any country. Communism is only possible when capitalism has been transformed into socialism in all countries. For the communist stage of economic and social development is defined as that period when salary and services will be distributed to workers on the basis of need rather than deed.

That, basically, is the theory of socialism. An examination of the practice of socialism in Cuba will give a much better picture of how it has worked and how it has not worked.

One of the first things that the Castro government did, several years before Cuban society became socialist, was to confiscate property which had been illegally accumulated during the decades of corrupt government, as typified by Machado and Batista. The largest single haul came, in fact, from the Batista family itself, most of whose members fled the island as soon as the rebel forces won. It was discovered that in addition to the money which Batista had carefully hoarded in Swiss and American banks, he had left in Cuban banks safety deposit boxes containing millions of pesos (the Cuban peso is worth one dollar). One box alone held 1.1 million pesos, all in thousand-peso bills. In addition to hard cash, Batista owned, directly or indirectly, large sugar refineries and lands, and the total worth of the property confiscated from him and his family came to 3 million in cash and at least 30 million in stocks and bonds, not counting his refinery and his farm.

In other words, while over 60 percent of the population was uneducated, for example, Batista and his high officials were accumulating private treasures from private industries and national funds for their own personal use. Not only Batista did this; other members of the government, wealthy Cuban and American businessmen, gambling syndicates—all used the wealth of the country for their own ends. Many built luxurious mansions and country clubs; others invested in first-class hotels and casinos; still others turned to the raising of cattle—whatever their activities, they used the profits for their own enjoyment, and few of the millions and millions of pesos were translated into programs which would benefit the people.

These private fortunes were used to purchase items of tremendous luxury. The women collected fabulous jewels, one ring alone being valued at forty-five thousand dollars. Batista's son Papo owned a lovely fan, made of solid eighteen-karat gold, encrusted with diamonds and adorned with delicate Brussels lace—the fan, of course, was useless for anything but display, for it weighed too much to be used. Not to be outdone, his father had a solid gold chamber pot, while the provisional president Andrés Domingo preferred an enameled toilet seat dotted with gold fleurs-de-lys, and another man luxuriated in a massive gold-plated bed. Between the jewels, the silverware, the velvet and lace, the planes and limousines, the yachts and mansions, the lands and industries, the forty-five thousand head of cattle, the mammoth marble mausoleums, the radio stations and newspapers, these men and women, a tiny percentage of the total population, were worth over $400 million.

When the Castro government took over all this wealth, it was immediately distributed among the most essential new government programs: agrarian reform, public works, housing, social security, and education. One might wonder why these new politicians behaved differently from their predecessors, why Castro and company did not simply take over all the riches left by the previous regime for their personal use. The fact is that, whatever else they might be, the men and women who govern Cuba, beginning with Castro himself, are meticulously honest, something on which all observers have agreed. Most of them, in fact, prefer to lead austere and frugal lives, eschewing any semblance of luxury.

After these funds were made available for public services, the government then faced what was perhaps its greatest problem: how to rebuild its entire economy. Sugar had been for centuries one of the two crops that Cuba cultivated in large quantities. Sugar was the basic commodity that Cuba traded with the United States; sugar was the product that brought in most of the money the government had. The economy before the revolution was dominated by sugar, and so was life on the island. In those early days in 1959, there was massive public sentiment of disgust and resentment against sugar and everything it had stood for, and there was also the realization that if the new government wanted to develop a country economically and politically independent of all other countries, other agricultural products must be cultivated and new industries set up.

This led to the early and rather drastic plans for diversification of the economy, whereby less sugar would be produced and more attention given to other aspects of production. The change became a vital necessity once the United States began to cut off trade with Cuba, for up until 1961 Cuba had imported virtually everything from its neighbor to the north. This meant that Cubans depended on the United States for everything: under- and over-wear; canned foods of all kinds; fresh vegetables and fruits; fish and meat; medicines and medical equipment; books, magazines, and films; heavy and light machinery; electrical appliances, from refrigerators to shavers; toothbrushes and all cosmetics; cars, trucks, and boats; elevators and air conditioners; rice and beans; toilet paper and cigarettes; pencils, paper, and typewriters; liquor and sodas; towels, cameras, ink, hats, and pins; bread, ice cream, and even candy. American interests owned seventy-five thousand acres of Cuban land, the major utilities companies (electricity and telephone and water), and the largest factories and refineries. In other words, Cubans of all walks of life depended on the United States indirectly or directly for almost every aspect of their existence, from work to entertainment, from education to health services.

The task of the Castro government, then, if it wished to become economically independent, was to make it possible for all these items and more to be produced in Cuba by Cuban industries. Some of the earliest factories produced textiles, canned tomatoes, pencils, and dolls; later on, brushes of all kinds, baseballs, refrigerators, and stoves were also produced locally. By now many other items are Cuban-made. But the job of converting an economy from a mono-culture (based on one crop) to a healthy diversified one is long and difficult, and to date Cuba is still forced to import many essential commodities from other countries, and to continue producing large quantities of sugar to trade.

When rents were reduced by 50 percent in 1959 and subsequently to 10 percent of the tenant's salary (with many people now paying no rent at all), when water and public telephones were provided at

Farm workers' housing in an agricultural cooperative.

no cost, when health and educational services became available free (almost immediately after the revolution), and when wages and salaries for the mass of the people were raised, the demand for consumer goods became tremendous. With so many essentials provided free of charge, and with more money being paid them, the average Cubans were able finally to buy things they had never before owned. This tremendous increase in demand, and the inability of the economy to satisfy it at once for lack of resources and industries, is at the root of the shortages about which we read so frequently. The fact is that even before the revolution there were severe shortages, but because 85 percent of the population was unable to even consider buying things, the shortages were not apparent. If there were thousands of dresses available in a store before, it was primarily because only a very few could buy them, and the bulk of the population had to make do with rags. Once this majority was given purchasing power, they, too, were able to buy, and then the shortage appeared. In order to guarantee that every Cuban would get the food, clothing, and other essentials necessary for a healthy life, most items are rationed to assure equal distribution.

Another change which took place in the Cuban economy quite early had to do with trading partners. Again, during the half century preceding the revolution, Cuba had traded almost exclusively with the United States, and this relationship was seen by the revolutionary leadership as one of the major sources of Cuba's ills. Therefore, the new government sought new trading partners, and was in fact forced to do so, as the United States embargoed trade and cut the sugar quota. For quite a while only the countries in the socialist bloc would trade with Cuba, and that is one reason why the island has established such close commercial and cultural ties with Russia, China, and others. Eventually, Spain, Japan, Belgium, Great Britain, Canada, and other nations of the "free world" established normal commercial relations with the Castro government.

The early years of massive diversification proved to be an example of mistaken planning for the Cuban economy, for without sugar and cattle, tobacco and coffee as major exports, Cuba could not earn the income needed to construct millions of housing units, to finance massive programs in public health and education, to establish factories providing commodities and farms providing food. Thus, in 1962 the economy shifted back to an emphasis on sugar and cattle particularly, since these two products were traditional Cuban exports and could provide the basis for the other programs planned by the government.

This does not mean, however, that the development of other areas of the society has been underemphasized. On the contrary, with the income from sugar and cattle the government has been able to go ahead with many other projects. Housing continues to be one of the most urgent needs in Cuba, even with the massive construction of urban and rural housing developments. New ways have been developed to speed up the process of providing comfortable and sturdy living quarters, beginning with temporary measures of repair and renovation, and including also programs like the "Plan Alamar." In this case skilled workers from various factories in an area were selected to leave their jobs and work only on the construction of a new city in which they and their families would eventually live. Alamar, a few miles out of Havana, was built entirely by the men and women who later inhabited it. When fully completed, the city will have adequate schools (some are already built for the children now living there), a shoe factory, a furniture factory, a refinery, a sports complex, administrative buildings, apartments and small houses, and all the other elements of a small city.

Health, to which the Cuban government has devoted millions of pesos and countless hours of work and planning, is one of the most spectacular areas of change in Cuban society. The national health budget before the revolution was 21 million pesos a year; in 1967 it was up to 158 million pesos a year. Where fifty-one people out of every one hundred thousand annually suffered from gastroenteritis (a severe intestinal disease affecting mostly children), by 1966 only nineteen did; polio, once a major child-killer, has not appeared in

Cuba since 1968; in the 1950s there were from seven thousand to ten thousand cases of malaria annually, and in 1967 there were only ten cases.

In 1958 there was one medical school on the island, 57 hospitals in the several large cities, one rural hospital for the total peasant population; Cuba had not one public dental clinic, and most doctors went immediately into private practice upon graduation. By 1968, there were three medical schools and several teaching hospitals, 170 hospitals and 250 clinics in the cities, and 47 hospitals and 50 or more medical and dental clinics in the countryside.

While close to one-half of Cuban doctors left after the revolution, there are still more doctors today—7,000—than there were before 1959. Even though only 17 of the 158 senior professors at the medical school of the University of Havana stayed after 1959, there are by now enough professors to teach in the three medical schools. Where there were only 20 qualified pathologists on the entire island in 1958, and only 9 remained after the revolution, by 1968 there were well over 60, and by now there are close to 100.

One of the reasons so many of the doctors and professors left is that today private medical practice is virtually nonexistent. All medical students must spend the first two years after graduation working in hospitals, clinics, and dispensaries in the countryside, and many continue there permanently. The few doctors who remained after the revolution continue to receive the same salaries as before, but the maximum salary which any new doctor can receive is 750 pesos a month; he or she also gets one month's vacation a year (as do all Cuban workers), and of course, along with the rest of the population, doctors receive free health care and education. Their rent is 10 percent or less of their salary, and essentials like food and clothing are relatively cheap.

Cuban medicine today is characterized by its emphasis on prevention rather than cure; that is, most funds and research are devoted to programs to train people in personal hygiene, to teach previously uneducated peasants healthy living habits, to encourage all Cubans to keep fit through a combined program of healthy eating and energetic participation in sports and other physical activities. The goal is to eliminate traditionally epidemic diseases so that less time and money will have to be spent in the future curing them.

There are, of course, many things being done in the curing aspects of medicine also. Despite the shortage of medicines, equipment, and trained personnel, the Cardiovascular Institute, for example, was able successfully to perform 850 closed and open heart operations and to implant over 50 pacemakers between 1965 and 1968.

The island's largest state mental institution, Mazorra, before the revolution was one of the worst examples of medieval and inhumane treatment of the mentally ill. Today it is a productive and attractive place, with new living quarters, a baseball stadium, an outdoor movie theater, and art studios and workshops. The most modern approaches to mental illness are used. The majority of the patients are able to work productively and they run one of Cuba's largest scientific chicken farms. There are no guards or fences, and all visitors have been impressed by the high level of contentment and creativity among most of the patients.

Thus, in Cuba today *all* aspects of health care are completely free to all Cubans, from an annual checkup to open heart surgery, from teeth-cleaning to psychotherapy, from painkillers to insulin. The country's economy is building industry and agriculture, is attempting to rapidly provide adequate housing where it is needed, and in general the government seems to have done remarkably well in changing the lives of the Cuban people—especially well in the light of the tremendous social and economic problems which faced them in 1959, and the political and economic problems which have arisen since then. But the area of most spectacular success is in education.

10

The Future Belongs to the Young

If you know, teach; if you don't know, learn.

Slogan, 1961, Year of Education

In the foothills of the Sierra Maestra, miles from the nearest small town, lived a family named Morales. Genovevo and Rosario, both descended from generations of peasants, shared their two-room *bohío* with their six children, and together the family just barely managed to eke out a living. Genovevo was a cane cutter when the season permitted: four months out of the year he would leave his family to harvest the sugarcane, bringing back the meager wage he earned, on which the entire family was supposed to live for the rest of the year. To supplement this the three oldest boys hired out as day laborers, weeding cane fields, planting pasturage, and doing whatever job the season and the economy would allow. More often than not they were idle, spending their time hunting in the forest of the sierra in the hopes of bringing home some small game. Rosario, already old at thirty-two, tended a tiny plot of land behind the hut where she grew a few sickly greens. The whole family showed signs of malnutrition and disease; two children had died over the years from gastroenteritis, and one at birth; the nearest doctor was over two days' walking distance, and in any case medical care was much too expensive for the family. The nearest school was even farther away, in Santiago, and no member of the family had ever been inside it, let alone held a book.

In 1958, fifteen-year-old Ciro ran away to join Fidel in the mountains. Genovevo and Rosario were indifferent to their son's reasons for leaving at first, for what did they know of politics? Hadn't they both lived through governmental changes already, and what good had it done them? They still lived in abject misery, they still had to scrounge for food, they still had to watch their infants sicken and die, and no one yet had offered any of them a rosy future. On the two visits Ciro paid them before he was killed by the army he tried to tell them about the *barbudos,* those bearded men with whom he was fighting, about the schools they were planning, about their ideas for the new Cuba. Genovevo would shake his head sadly, secretly admiring his son's enthusiasm, but all too familiar with hopes shattered and promises broken. Rosario had too many worries to concern herself with her son's chattering—she only hoped he would live and be happy, and maybe those *barbudos* would fix him up with a good job.

But things changed for the Morales family quite rapidly after January 1, 1959. In the two short years which followed, a clinic and dispensary were built no more than an hour's walk away, and for the first time in their lives the Morales' were examined by a doctor and treated for their various ailments. On the heels of this unexpected miracle, Genovevo's wages were raised considerably and he was soon persuaded to work at the sugar refinery during the off season. Suddenly the family had money to spend year-round, not much, but significantly more than they had ever seen at one time.

Not only that, but they were eating well for the first time. Like all Cuban families they received, at a moderate price, eggs and a quarter of a pound of meat per person weekly, a liter (a little over a quart) of milk every day for each child, and even a chicken once a month, plus an adequate ration of sugar, salt, beans, rice, and flour. Occasionally they had fresh fruit and vegetables. At first this new diet was strange: Genovevo remembered having once eaten chicken at his younger sister's wedding, but none of the family had ever tasted beef, and the children had found the white liquid they now drank mysterious and awesome at first.

Under the government's rationing system they were also entitled to buy, again at low cost, all sorts of clothing: two pairs of leather shoes each, two pairs of sandals, a pair of tennis shoes, adequate dress clothes and work clothes, underwear and outerwear, and many meters of fabric annually. The biggest source of early amazement and amusement were the brassieres, for neither Rosario nor her daughters had ever seen one. Shoes were hard to get used to, after years of going barefoot.

Before they had quite recovered from these early shocks they were visited, in 1961, by a young man (a boy, really, for he was only sixteen, hardly older than Tomás) who told them he was there to teach the whole family to read and write. A high school student, he was one of the three hundred thousand Cubans from age ten to sixty who worked as volunteers in the government's massive literacy campaign.

This campaign, for which Cuba is now world-renowned, had as its goal the elimination of all illiteracy on the island in one year. An ambitious task, since close to one-quarter of the population could neither read nor write. Schoolchildren and university students, teachers, doctors and lawyers, factory and office workers, anyone who could read and write was called on to volunteer some time to teach these skills to others. The professional educators served as planners and supervisors, and the rest as teachers.

Not only were the Morales taught reading and writing (Genovevo was taught at the refinery and the rest of the family at home) but they were also taught basic hygiene, nutrition, and other elementary but essential subjects which would make their lives better. By the end of 1961 the seven members of the Morales family were part of the enormous group of Cubans who were now basically literate;

University students between classes.

although many people had felt that the original goal would not be achieved, in one year illiteracy was virtually eradicated, and only 3.9 percent of all Cubans were still unable to read or write—these few were counted primarily among the mentally ill and the aged. So astonishing were these results that even UNESCO (the United Nations Education, Scientific and Cultural Organization) held up the Cuban experience as a model for other less developed countries.

Early in 1962 a new town was built near the sugar refinery, with housing, stores, schools, and recreation centers. Because Genovevo had participated in the construction, the Morales were one of the first families to move in, and they were given, rent-free, a little blue house with two bedrooms in addition to the living room, kitchen, and inside bathroom. More surprises, for they had never before seen electric lights, running water, or a toilet in a person's home.

While six-year-old Lucita lived at home and attended the brand-new primary school, the other children became *becados* (scholarship boarding students) and joined the 250,000 other students (mostly from peasant families) who were housed in the mansions of Miramar. They went to schools in Havana and were soon to complete their elementary education and go on to high school. Life as *becados* was full of newness and surprises, for none of the Morales children had ever been in a city, and they were wide-eyed with wonder at all the new things they saw and experienced: movies, theater, ballet, the beaches, the skyscrapers and crowded streets, the thousands of other children studying and learning new things daily. In addition to their schooling, which was entirely free (as are all levels of school for all Cubans of all ages), they were boarded and fed at no cost to their family, and their clothing, their books, and spending money were also provided by the government.

Meanwhile, Rosario had become intrigued with education now that she could read and write; she realized how much there was for her to learn and wanted to continue her education. But how could a thirty-five-year-old woman like her, with five children living and four more whom she had buried, sit in a schoolroom with youngsters and show her ignorance? She was much too embarrassed to even try, but it turned out that she was not the only one. Shortly after the family moved to its new home, she joined a small group of other women in the same predicament. This group, like hundreds of similar groups throughout the island, was organized by the Federation of Cuban Women; they met several times a week with a teacher and began the difficult but stimulating job of finishing their primary education. At the same time her husband was learning also, at the refinery where before work, during lunch hour, and for a few hours in the afternoon the men that wanted to could catch up on what they had missed. This meant that all seven members of the family were to reach at least a sixth-grade level in their education, a situation which none of them would have even contemplated before 1959.

Hortensia, the eighteen-year-old daughter, had enrolled in a training program which would prepare her to work in the local textile factory. Her classes also included primary education, but what interested her most was that she would acquire a skill that would free her from economic dependence on her parents. As part of her training she worked periodically at different jobs in the factory nearby to determine which particular one best suited her. After her training she was able to start to work right away, while she continued her education in the evenings.

The adult Morales were used to hard and unremitting work, and therefore were pleasantly surprised when they realized that they, like all workers in Cuba, were entitled to a month's vacation each year. They were now able to visit resort areas and cities which they had perhaps heard about but had never seen: Varadero and Guardalabarca, Holguín and Santa Clara. It was, in fact, in Santa Clara that Hortensia met Claudio Arce, a young construction worker in that city. After a brief courtship they decided to marry, and the entire family celebrated the wedding with refreshments and entertainment provided at very low cost by the government. The young couple stayed in Santa Clara where Hortensia joined a program that would train her to be a day care worker, for she had always enjoyed small children.

In Havana, the younger Morales were progressing well. In seventh grade Antonio decided he would like to be a teacher and he signed up for the rigorous five-year course in elementary education. His first year was spent back home—that is, at a school on the peak of a mountain in the Sierra Maestra. Here, at Minas del Frío, the students live ruggedly, in order to prepare them for teaching in the remote rural regions where most of the teachers are needed. They lived at first in primitive camplike conditions until the buildings were completed. Even now, life there is more like a camping trip than a boarding school as we know it. But the curriculum for the students is a familiar one: botany, geography, history, math, Spanish, and physical education.

Antonio (and all other students following the same course of study) spent the eighth- and ninth-grade years at another school, the Manuel Ascunce Domenech School in Topes, Las Villas Province. This school too is in the remote countryside, and when Antonio went there it was not yet completed. So the students, in addition to a pretty heavy academic schedule, helped in the necessary construction work on campus. They studied the same subjects as before, but in their second year at Topes courses in pedagogy, or education, were added, as well as physics and art.

When the two years at Topes were over, Antonio went on to the Makarenko Pedagogical Institute, located outside Havana. Here

Students building their own school.

the emphasis is more and more on pedagogy, with ample opportunities for practice teaching: every morning the tenth-grade students teach first through fourth grades in schools in Havana Province, while the eleventh-graders teach fifth and sixth grades. In the afternoons and evenings they have classes and study.

With this concentrated program in teacher training, Cuba has been able to graduate enough new teachers not only to replace the teachers who left but also to meet the greatly expanded demand for education on the island.

Because Cuba became so soon a country at study—by 1962 eight out of ten children, for example, were enrolled in schools, and by 1968 over five hundred thousand adults were involved in adult education of one kind or another—it was not surprising that Genovevo and Rosario also decided to continue their schooling. At the refinery Genovevo trained for more skilled jobs and was able to reach a higher level of preparation and earn a higher salary than he had ever dreamed of. Rosario, inspired by Hortensia's work at the textile factory, enrolled in the same program that had trained her daughter and was soon going to work every day. She decided to do this in 1964, when her youngest child, Ernestina, was still an infant. Not only was Ernestina the first of the Morales children to be delivered in a hospital, but she was also the only one who was still little enough to go to the local day care center, constructed after the revolution. When Ernestina was forty-five days old, Rosario had started taking her there for the day. Rosario was then able to go to work with an easy mind, for she knew that the child would be well cared for at the center.

Lucita was also completing her primary education. When she finished sixth grade she heard about the Island of Youth (formerly the Isle of Pines) and decided to go there. Undercultivated, underpopulated, and devastated by a hurricane in 1966, the island became the site of a fascinating and so far successful experiment in living. Secondary and university students from all over the island volunteered to go there, either for two years or permanently, to work and study and live. They repaired the damage caused by the hurricane, built new farms and communities, worked the land, harvested the citrus crop, raised the livestock, administered the egg farm, and all in all ran the entire island. Lucita had originally planned to stay for only two years, but after completing ninth grade and working on the livestock farm, she decided to make Isla de la Juventud her home.

While all the Morales children were in school they, like all other Cuban schoolchildren, spent six weeks a year working in the country as part of the "School Goes to the Countryside" program instituted by the Ministry of Education. This program not only provides desperately needed help during the harvest, for example, but it also gives the students the opportunity to live a different kind of life. For Tomás, Jorge Luis, and Antonio Morales country life was not new, but they did discover all sorts of things about planned agricul-

Students on their way to the countryside.

ture and livestock breeding which they had not known before. These experiences led Jorge Luis to choose agronomy as his future career.

Today, in 1973, the entire Morales family is continuing to learn, and its younger members in particular are benefitting tangibly from the new government policies. Hortensia is a trained day care worker in Santa Clara, and because the government has realized that the workers at the centers must be much better educated than was originally thought, she continues to go to classes after work. Her new course of study includes basic child psychology, nutrition and health, early childhood development—all planned and coordinated by the Children's Institute which was founded in 1971. She was encouraged to enroll by a friend of hers who had joined the Federation of Cuban Women with her in 1968.

Tomás is now married, has one child, and works in a furniture factory in the new city of Alamar. His wife works in the shoe factory, and they live in an apartment in one of the buildings just recently completed. They have both finished their elementary education, have received special training for the jobs they now hold, and plan to continue going to school in order to complete high school.

Jorge Luis is at the University in Santiago de Cuba studying agronomy, and plans to work with the Ministry of Agriculture when he graduates. Antonio teaches fifth grade in Camaguey Province, in a small and modern rural school which was not there before 1959.

Lucita is still on the Isla de la Juventud, along with the thirty thousand other new and youthful inhabitants. She plans to marry a fellow student who came to the island when she did. Like many young couples there, they have worked together on the construction of a new town for married couples, since they are not the only ones who have decided to stay there and raise a family. While they work on the housing, others are building schools for the next generations. Lucita will shortly go to Havana for a few years in order to complete her studies in veterinary medicine, a profession which she will then practice on one of the island's livestock farms.

Ernestina is almost ten now and lives in Santa Clara with her sister Hortensia. She is an enthusiastic member of a local "Interest Circle," a network of informal groups formed to stimulate an interest in things scientific and technical among elementary school children. Last year she exhibited her project on rain and clouds, accompanying her graphs and drawings with a clear and intelligent lecture. Although she likes science, she is also attracted to art, after having seen several shows and exhibits in the Santa Clara museums. She might in fact try out for the art school at Cubanacán, outside of Havana, but she does not have to decide immediately.

The Morales family is by no means atypical in today's Cuba. While as poor peasants they had no future to look forward to before 1959, since the revolution they have been able to better themselves, to rise to higher positions, and to develop a sense of contribution and productivity. Being not only poor but also mulatto, their experience since 1959 has been especially important. Before the revolution black and mulatto children were barred from higher education (by tradition if not by law), and it was unheard of that one such family should produce children who would enter such a variety of occupations and professions.

The fact is that the Cuban government is realizing the tremendous importance of education at all levels for all Cubans, for only that way can the Cuban people contribute fully to the building and maintenance of their society. That is why, through the multiple programs offered, through massive campaigns of one sort or another, 27.5 percent or more of all Cubans, adults and children, black and white, are enrolled in some kind of school. This is the highest percentage in all of Latin America, and has markedly raised the general cultural and technological levels of the people. Although the story of the Morales family is fictitious, it is a reality for thousands and thousands of Cuban families whose vistas have been immeasurably broadened and whose children and grandchildren can contemplate wide-open futures where their individual talents and interests, rather than the harsh laws of poverty and prejudice, will dictate what they make of their lives.

11

Cubanas, Past and Present

For us, the liberation of women cannot be separated from the liberation of all of society.

Vilma Espin
President, Federation of Cuban Women

"Sitting in dark and tranquil corners in their homes, women have patiently waited for this sublime hour in which a revolution would come to remove their yokes and untie their wings. . . .

"When the time comes to liberate women, the Cuban men who have eradicated the slavery of color will also devote their energies to the conquest of the rights of those who today, in this war, are their sisters of charity and who have been and always will be their exemplary comrades."

These words were spoken in April, 1869, by the Cuban feminist leader Ana Betancourt de Mora. She was addressing members of the revolutionary constitutional assembly who had gathered to formulate the constitution which would govern Cuba once the island was freed from Spanish rule. Her words are significant for several reasons; first, it is of historical importance to realize that the movement to grant women greater participation in the life of their country was apparently quite alive in the Cuba of one hundred years ago; more importantly, in her last phrase Ana Betancourt reveals that in fact Cuban women had long since been struggling side by side with men in the various movements for social and political freedom.

A voyage through history shows us that this was indeed the case. As early as the Indian uprisings in the early sixteenth century the Indian woman Habaguanex is recorded as having led, with her husband, an abortive attempt to expel the Spanish invaders. One wonders about the countless, nameless slave women who in like moments must have fought with the male slaves, and fled with them to the *palenques* in the sierra in order to live free.

It is strange to note that while Cuban women, like their sisters throughout the South American continent, were subjugated by the rigid and conservative social forces developed over centuries of Spanish Catholic training, there were in fact numerous women who broke out of the mold and who stood out as modern, freethinking citizens, interested and active in the vital and often dangerous movements in which patriotic Cubans were involved. We have seen that when the "Bronze Titan" Antonio Maceo took to the mountains to join the struggle for independence he was accompanied by his wife, María Cabrales de Maceo, who served as a nurse in the revolutionary camp, and gave birth to a child during wartime, and his mother, Mariana Grajales, who also joined the rebels as a nurse and was to see her sons and husband die in battle—today she is known as the Mother of the Nation.

One of the most beloved heroines of the wars for independence was the ex-slave woman Rosa Castellanos, who joined the struggle as early as 1868, shortly after the Grito de Yara. She brought with her the vital knowledge of folk medicine and used her familiarity with curative plants and herbs to tend the sick and wounded. In

Mariana Grajales,
mother of Antonio Maceo.

1895 she established a blood bank in Camaguey Province, and for her valiant work during the war General Máximo Gómez named her a captain in the liberating army. Despite her life of danger and struggle, she lived to be seventy-three years old.

Many women worked as nurses and aides in the *mambiso* camps; many others fought side by side with the men. Some of them came with their entire families, others remained in the cities organizing secretly to recruit soldiers, collect funds and supplies, and lead demonstrations. Among the most notable women of the period were Captain Luz Palomares García, who lived to be ninety-eight years old; Candelaria Figuerado, who at the age of sixteen led the march on Bayamo, with her father's blessing; Ana Betancourt, who, aside from verbalizing feminist ideals, fought actively in the war; Fernanda Toro Pelegrín, the wife of General Máximo Gómez, who lived with him in the rebel camps; Lieutenant María Hidalgo Santana, who received seven wounds in one battle alone; Isabel Rubio Díaz, who with her husband and son joined the rebels as a fighter and a nurse, and at sixty set up a blood bank—she was shot in front of the hospital by invading Spanish forces and died two days later;

Captain Adela Azcuy Labrador, a young woman from a wealthy family and a veteran of forty-nine battles; and many, many more.

While Cuban women fought both openly and clandestinely against the various tyrannical governments that followed the winning of independence from Spain, the state did nothing to change the lot of women until the constitution of 1940, which declared discrimination on the basis of sex or race illegal and greatly liberalized marriage and divorce laws. Nevertheless, this was merely a paper concession, and the life of the Cuban woman changed very little in reality. The wealthier women continued to lead lives of idleness and frustration in their homes. For the peasant and working women life was not so gracious; on the contrary, while these women were subjected to the same intolerable social and economic conditions as their men, they were doubly exploited in that their own society saw them as inferior to even the poorest man.

Somehow, many women managed during the Machado and Batista periods to come to the forefront of political activities, gaining reputations as firm and dedicated fighters for social justice. These women, like those who participated in the independence struggles, came from a variety of social and economic backgrounds. América Labadí Arce was from a working family and was killed by the Machado forces during a demonstration at the age of twenty-six; Urselia Díaz Báez was a high school student in Havana and a member of the revolutionary movement, dying at eighteen on a suicide mission of sabotage; Lidia Doce Sánchez was a forty-five-year-old peasant woman, a baker, who joined the guerrillas in the Sierra Maestra and was Che Guevara's most trusted and courageous courier; Clodomira Acosta Ferrals was a black peasant woman from Oriente who became Fidel Castro's courier and along with Lidia Doce was captured by the Batista forces, tortured, and killed in 1958.

Among the early and present revolutionary leadership are several outstanding women who took their places with the men and fought as hard and as bravely as they. Haydée (or Yeyé) Santamaría and Melba Hernández were the two women involved in the attack on the Moncada barracks. Along with the other survivors of the incident they were imprisoned and tortured, but lived to join the struggle in the sierra and to see the triumph of the revolution. Today Haydée is a minister of the Politburo, a member of the central committee of the Communist party of Cuba, and head of the national publishing house and cultural center; Melba is the president of a major governmental agency.

Celia Sánchez is perhaps one of the best-known figures of the Cuban Revolution. She was one of the few city women who joined the fighting in the sierra as early as 1957, and since those days has been considered Castro's right hand. She is a close associate and confidante, next only to his brother Raúl and his physician René Vallejo, and is presently minister of the presidency. She is reputed to be a warm and humorous woman, slight, active, and a meticulous dresser, although she is rarely seen in anything but army fatigues.

Vilma Espín is the founder and president of the Federation of Cuban Women. An engineering student in the 1950s—with two years of study at the Massachusetts Institute of Technology—she worked with Frank País in organizing the assault on Moncada, and also organized the underground which would back up the guerrillas once they reached the sierra. She fought alongside Raúl Castro on the Second Eastern Front during the revolution and they were married a few weeks after the victory. She is now one of the two women on the central committee.

It should be clear that the success of the various revolutionary struggles in Cuba is due in no small part to the role that women played during those periods. The revolutionary leaders had recognized early that for the revolution to succeed and be maintained, the specific problems of Cuban women had to be tackled from the beginning and their contributions sought out and cultivated. This approach was valuable, as attested to by the performance of the women who joined the guerrillas. The experience with these female comrades led Guevara to include, in his handbook on guerrilla warfare, a section on the role of the woman in the guerrilla front. He wrote: "The woman is capable of performing the most difficult tasks, of fighting beside the man; and, despite current belief, she

Vilma Espín, president of the Federation of Cuban Women.

does not create conflicts of a sexual type in the troops. In the rigorous combatant life, the woman is a companion who brings the qualities appropriate to her sex, but she can work the same as a man and she can fight; she is weaker, but no less resistant than he."

The theoretical acceptance of an equal role for women in a revolutionary society, and the direct experience with the women in the Sierra, led to clearly defined programs which were established as soon as the fighting ended. These programs are not administered by men; rather, leadership and responsibility are delegated to the women themselves.

One of the earliest such programs was the rehabilitation of prostitutes. As has been mentioned earlier, Cuba suffered greatly from this particular social problem, and when the revolution was over the government was faced with the question of what to do about the thousands of girls and women—reputedly up to fifteen thousand in Havana alone—whose lives had been devoted to the "oldest profession." A program of education and rehabilitation was set up, allowing the women to train for jobs. They were taught general literacy and also given a political education; then they were trained in various fields, preparing them for factory, office, or agricultural work. Those who wanted to could graduate from these special schools and enter the regular school system, continuing into higher education in order to study for a profession. The program was entirely voluntary, although there must have been a great deal of social pressure on the women to join it and better themselves. A few of these women left the country in the early months after the revolution, but the majority who chose to retrain were given jobs, once their studies were over, in regions far enough away from their old homes so as not to present unnecessary conflicts. For a while they were visited by social workers, and eventually were left to pursue productive lives as respected members of society.

Similar retraining programs were established for domestic workers and peasant women who wished to prepare themselves for different work and to receive a complete general education at the same time.

The underlying theme of the Cuban government's programs for women is their complete integration into the productive society. This is being achieved not only by the special training programs, but also by the opening up of jobs previously limited to men, the expansion of educational opportunities for women, and their participation in the militia.

In order to do this, special projects have been necessary. Agricultural schools for women have sprouted up all over the island, each quite small in itself, but the totality representing a vast change in the traditional division of labor. There are also poultry schools, horticultural schools, animal husbandry schools—all specifically for women.

In addition to moving women into skilled agriculture, programs have opened up nonagricultural jobs to them, as well as jobs in industries which are linked to agriculture. Thus, in Havana, special schools were established to train women in cigar making, a job which was traditionally open to men only. By the end of 1968 more than ten thousand women were working in that industry.

Bank personnel were slowly shifted, so that by now most banks are worked entirely by women. Nearly 50 percent of the students in the universities are women; up to 90 percent of the students in education, 50 percent in medicine, and 30 percent in engineering are women. The programs for 1972/73 include the attempt to incorporate more nonworking housewives into the productive society by educating them, training them, and encouraging them to do volunteer agricultural or office work. Over four hundred thousand housewives are expected to voluntarily join small study groups, and about twenty-seven thousand will enroll in formal adult education courses. Thousands of women have replaced male workers in the sugar mills; one hundred or more Havana bus drivers are now women; there are increasing numbers of female traffic police; women run countless vegetable gardens and fruit orchards around Havana (the Havana Green Belt) which provide the city with the fresh food that it needs; many others have entered the burgeoning handicrafts industry.

Young women training to be gymnasts.

A fundamental reason for the success of the programs is the existence of corollary programs to handle the problem of the children of working mothers. A network of day care centers was developed quite early in the days following January 1, 1959, and more are being constructed each year. The centers provide day-long (sometimes night-long or twenty-four-hour) care for children whose mothers work. Children are accepted from the age of forty-five days and are kept until they are ready for school. They are brought every morning before work and are picked up again in the evening. Not only are these centers free, but they also provide free food, clothing, and medical attention, and preschooling for the older children. Although hundreds more such centers are desperately needed, it is now infinitely easier for most Cuban women to become working members of their society.

Women can now also participate in a variety of areas of civic life. In fact, women in Cuba are playing a very important role in many phases of politics, culture, and education. Although military service is not compulsory for women (except in the universities, where all students get some military instruction) there are quite a few female paratroopers in the Revolutionary Armed Forces, and a large majority of younger women are in the voluntary militia and stand their guard duty, day or night, along with the men.

An organization in which women are perhaps more important than men is the network of "Committees for the Defense of the Revolution." These groups are organized on a block-by-block basis in each urban and rural population center. They serve as a vehicle for bringing government programs (health, educational, and political) to the people. Vaccination campaigns, for example, are in large part successful because the women in the committees—mostly women who do not work outside the home—go from door to door urging the people to take their entire families to the clinics.

In the area of job opportunities, then, the Cuban government has made tremendous advances with regard to women. By opening up new jobs, by training women for new professions, and by providing day care for children, it has made it more feasible for women to work and improve themselves. In less tangible ways the government has also begun to move against the carry-overs of traditional male chauvinism or *machismo* in Cuba. While in previous regimes the laws on the books were rarely upheld, in today's Cuba they are rigorously maintained. Thus, for example, it is not seen as adequate simply to legislate against job discrimination; there is a system whereby an available job must be given to a qualified woman applicant over an equally qualified male, in order to encourage more women to enter fields previously closed to them and to help men become used to

Billboard urges women to participate in the sugar harvest.

the idea that women may qualify as well or better for the same positions.

Marriage and divorce laws are extremely liberal, allowing very simple and low-cost procedures for both. Abortions are legal and are granted quite easily, and birth control is available to all women, married or single.

Naturally, social and personal attitudes are the slowest to change, and many Cubans, men and women alike, resist such radical alterations in traditional sex-based behavior patterns. There are men who resent having to look to female leadership; there are women who feel it is unnatural for them to assume certain new roles; there is a large problem of women who do not work outside the home and live instead off the work of others. Vilma Espín recently stated, "We still find discriminatory attitudes and some prejudices against women, and among women themselves."

But the most important element in making any changes possible has been the Cuban woman herself. Where the government has been slow or shortsighted, the women have demanded change loudly. They have thrust themselves into the work of the country with such a strong sense of purpose that their role has had to be accepted even by those who were reluctant to do so. Although they lived with the burden of centuries of poverty and subservience, Cuban women have broken into the world with such force that it is surprising even to the Cubans. Admitting his pleasant astonishment, Fidel Castro once said of Cuban women today: "We are finding that, in reality, their potential is superior to anything that the most optimistic of us ever dreamed."

12

Feeding the Mind and the Spirit

*Make the natural blood of the nation course and
throb through our veins!*

José Martí

While the kind of historical and cultural forces which have
shaped Cuban life may seem unfamiliar, while it may be difficult
to imagine living in Cuba today, it is important to remember that
Cubans are not so different from people anywhere. While their
customs and habits may be different, their basic interests and con-
cerns are not unlike our own. A hard-working, determined people—
honed over years of struggle and challenge—Cubans are also known
for their high spirits, their full-blooded relishing of play, their energy, and their humor. Cubans today not only work hard, they also
need time for relaxation and for contemplation. Like all people,
they seek a balance to their lives, a balance between times of concentrated effort and periods of leisurely enjoyment.

For many Cubans today religion is still a meaningful and important part of life, and the traditional Christian and Afro-Cuban

138

sects continue to practice their faiths with full freedom. While the number of people who attend church has diminished in the past few years—as it has in many other countries—the temples and churches of Cuba continue to fulfill their traditional roles, and to fill the spiritual needs of the Cubans.

Surprisingly enough, although there are no parochial schools, there are still several seminaries in Cuba, although immediately after the revolution many of the priests and pastors left the island. These seminaries, training future religious leaders, have increasingly become integrated into the fabric of socialist Cuba, and it does not seem an anachronism to anyone there that while some may be training to become agronomists or engineers, others should be preparing to enter the Catholic church or one of the Protestant churches.

Those men and women of the cloth who are presently in Cuba— there are Catholic archbishops, bishops, priests, and nuns; pastors of the Methodist, Baptist, Episcopalian, Presbyterian, and Evangelical faiths; and Jewish rabbis—have on many occasions expressed their support of the government's programs, especially those effecting vast educational and health reforms. Recently Monsignor Francisco Oves, archbishop of Havana, declared: "Our mission is to illuminate the conscience of Christians so that they live life more in accord with their faith, and to help them assume energetically their responsibility to participate in the construction of this new society, recognizing those human and evangelical values which are common both to Christianity and to socialism in our country, without neglecting the preservation of the fundamental rights of a strict religious conscience."

The recognized need for a new approach to religious faith and practice is mirrored in all aspects of Cuban cultural life. There is a general attempt to break with past conventions, many of which have been binding and restrictive, and to create new forms and new languages which can better answer the needs of today's Cubans. Even in an area like sports, where one might wonder how on earth baseball or fencing can be approached in a new and different way, the whole structure and emphasis have been altered significantly.

Because of the decades of American presence and influence, Cuban sports often developed in ways which were more suited to the United States than to Cuba. In part this development was welcomed: baseball, a United States import, is today the Cuban national sport. On the other hand, during the years of poverty and dictatorship, the importance of professional and amateur sports on the island was minimal, and most Cuban athletes found greater recognition in the United States than in their own country. Thus, some of Cuba's greatest ball players—Camilo Pascual and Pedro Ramos, to name two—actually played on American teams: the Washington Senators were well known during the 1940s and 1950s for their Cuban players. Athletes in other sports—track runners like Fortún, boxers like Miguel Angel González and "Kid Chocolate"—competed more often in Los Angeles or New York than in Santiago or Havana. Even the internationally known chess player José Raúl Capablanca was better known to American and European fans than to Cubans, and in fact he died in 1942 during a tournament in New York.

One thing the Castro government has done is to bring sports and athletes back home, to enable Cubans to excel in their various athletic fields on home territory. And more than this, the government has established a broad and popular program of physical fitness for all Cubans, encouraging participation in sports. All sports events are free to the spectators, and sports facilities for nonprofessionals are widely provided and easily accessible. Every new school, town, factory, community always has its own athletics complex—stadium, pool, track, game rooms, and equipment. The huge number of Cubans involved in sports—baseball, basketball, football, cycling, gymnastics, track, discus, tennis, boxing, volleyball, fencing, rowing, wrestling, swimming, and more—is astonishing when one considers that not long ago such activities were closed to the majority of Cubans.

Because of government encouragement, and because so many more Cubans now have the time and the means with which to practice sports, the level of performance of Cuban teams and athletes has risen sharply. At the Pan-American Games in 1971, held in Cali,

Basketball is a favorite sport of Cuban children.

Colombia, the Cuban athletes not only walked off with seven gold, six silver, and five bronze medals, but also managed to beat some of the traditionally superior teams who had till then been undefeated: they won against the American baseball, boxing, football, and volleyball teams, for example, something which had never happened before. In the 1972 Olympic Games Cuba won a total of eight medals: three gold, one silver, and four bronze. The three gold medals were in boxing, and the victories of the Cuban pugilists gave their team the world heavyweight championship. Cuba's overall performance in 1972 brought it to fourteenth place by the end of the games, whereas in the 1968 Olympics Cuba had placed thirty-first.

There is a new character to Cuban art and literature as well. In the first half of the twentieth century, Cubans were educated from American textbooks (if at all) and were taught to love and admire those great American and European figures to whom American children were also devoted. Little emphasis was placed on the study of the Cuban men and women who had contributed so fully to the island's own national culture, and more young Cubans could recite verses of Longfellow than of Julián del Casal, even though this poet is considered an important precursor of the modernist school. Nor were schoolchildren exposed to the rich and significant cultural contributions of their African forebears and their Afro-Cuban contemporaries.

Today Cuban literature is truly coming into its own. Now the country's great writers from the past are being studied and honored, and more contemporary authors and poets are being encouraged to create and develop a new, more characteristic national literary language. The novels of Alejo Carpentier, highly praised both in the United States and in Europe, sell thousands of copies in Cuba now, for the population is literate and hungry for works of high artistic merit. The short-story writers Noel Navarro, Virgilio Piñera, Calvert Casey, Ana María Simo, Humberto Arenal, Felix Pita Rodríguez, and others are being read with enthusiasm in Cuba as well as elsewhere.

Many of today's popular writers were in fact producing good work during the 1940s and 1950s, but were little known either in Cuba or abroad. Like many of these people, Cuba's poet laureate Nicolás Guillén is finally today receiving national and international acclaim. A mulatto born in 1902, Guillén contributed invaluably to the school of Afro-Cuban poetry, and has been compared to the black American poet Langston Hughes, whom Guillén knew personally and greatly admired. Hughes, on his part, was responsible for some of the earliest translations into English of Guillén's work. Like Hughes, Guillén is known for his simple, popular language, his concern with social and ethnic justice, and his pride in his diverse historical and social origins. His verse is often lilting and rhythmical, creating a sort of African musicality and tonality which so strongly characterizes his work. He writes most often of the simple men and women he has known, the Juans and Juanas of Cuba whose voices have so rarely been heard before.

The return to local and national themes and settings is seen in other aspects of Cuban culture. While Cuban popular music was all the rage in the United States during the three decades preceding the revolution, it did not receive the same kind of attention at home. The rumba and the conga, introduced into the world of entertainment by the Cuban composer and pianist Ernesto Lecuona, inspired dancing in the plush cabarets and dance halls in Havana, but the bulk of the Cuban population had never set foot in these places. While Americans swayed and wiggled to the rhythms of Xavier Cugat's Latin band, ordinary Cubans enjoyed the *sones,* the *puntos guajiros,* the *décimas,* and the *guaguancós* which were played and sung by unknown local balladeers in the remote regions of the countryside or in the poor neighborhoods of the cities.

Nicolás Guillén,
Cuba's poet laureate.

Today popular music and song are not cultivated for export, nor for the entertainment of foreign tourists. Those performers who for years went unnoticed in their own country, and those who were known only to their families and neighbors, now swell the ranks of the ever-growing field of popular entertainment.

Classical music, too, is finally reaching all the people, where before it was shared with only the educated and cultured. Composers like Leo Brouwer, Frank Fernández, and Rafael Somavilla now hear their works performed in great concert halls as well as in school auditoriums, in outdoor theaters, on makeshift platforms in the cane fields. Cuba's performers—the pianist Ivette Hernández, the Tiel brothers on piano and violin, for example—are beginning to be known not only in Cuba but internationally as well.

Mythological Personage by René Portocarrero (1945). Collection, The Museum of Modern Art, New York. Inter-American Fund.

Graphic arts also are entering a renascence, and where once the Cuban painters René Portocarrero and Wilfredo Lam were exhibited primarily in modern art museums and galleries in New York, Paris, and Stockholm, today their work is shown throughout Cuba. The art galleries in the cities are many and varied, displaying works which range from primitive to abstract expressionist, from representational to pop. Notably absent are works in the Soviet socialist-realist style. All over Cuba murals, canvases, sculptures, posters, collages, and mobiles are being produced, in a diversity of style, medium, and inspiration.

Young artists and musicians are graduating annually from the large art school at Cubanacán, built on the land which used to be Batista's private golf course. This complex of schools is not only architecturally exciting, but is also a good example of the government's approach to education. To Cubanacán come children from all parts of the island, from peasant families and from the families of professional people. Selected only on the basis of their talent and interest, these students receive high-level training in the various fields of art. Because all education is free in Cuba, and the government provides ample funds, the study of music, art, and dance is accessible to anyone of ability who wishes to pursue it.

At Cubanacán are the schools of classical ballet, folkloric ballet, and modern dance; the students who graduate from these schools are guaranteed positions as teachers in the school, or as dancers in one of the three national companies which are also subsidized by the government. What this means for a dancer can be clearly illustrated by Alicia Alonso's case.

Alicia Alonso is known throughout the world as one of the greatest prima ballerinas of this century. Although she trained initially as a child in Cuba during the 1930s, there was little opportunity there in those days for a girl with such talent, and she finished her training and made her professional debut in New York. There she danced for many years with the Ballet Theater, and it was during this time that she became famous for her favorite roles: Giselle, Odette/Odile, Princess Aurora, and Juliet. While she and

Alicia Alonso, prima ballerina of Cuba's National Ballet Company.

her choreographer husband Fernando made several attempts to establish and maintain a ballet company and a ballet school in Cuba, during the Batista period it was close to impossible to manage this financially. Thus, once again one of Cuba's best artists was better known by the rest of the world than by her compatriots.

After the revolution Alicia Alonso and her husband returned to Cuba and have lived and worked there ever since. With subsidies and encouragement from the government she directs the National Ballet Company and is deeply involved in the selection and training of ballet students at Cubanacán. Her company, considered one of the best in the world, is seen by Cubans in city and country alike.

Theater and ballet, folk and modern dance are favored entertainments in Cuba today; theaters are packed for a wide variety of productions, ranging from classical to light opera, from Renaissance to experimental drama, from tragedy to musical comedy. But the cinema continues to be the all-time favorite. During the decades preceding the revolution most movies seen by Cubans were made in Hollywood, and there is still a great fondness among Cubans for American westerns, Jerry Lewis comedies, and spine-chilling thrillers. The importation of American films is no longer permitted by the United States government, but the Cubans continue to return to the old films which they still have, and on occasion manage to receive newer ones. Thus, Paul Newman, Richard Burton, George Segal, Lee Remick, Jane Fonda, and a host of other stars have faithful fans in socialist Cuba.

Cuban cinematography is rapidly developing under the aegis of I.C.A.I.C., the Cuban Film Institute. Prior to 1959 the film industry in Cuba was small, and those movies which were made were, by and large, ignored—in fact, of the seventy films made there during the silent era, only five have survived. The institute is now building a comprehensive archive which will house and preserve all Cuban-made films, past and present. They also duplicate vast numbers of films, old and new, from around the world, and hope to develop one of the best film libraries in Latin America.

The Film Institute has theaters across the country that show films almost continuously to large and varied audiences. It runs a Cinema Museum where the history of the film industry is traced through exhibits. It encourages experimental film-making by the young, and these films are shown in the various studio theaters. The institute plans a major portion of Cuban television fare; organizes special film showings for schools, factories, farm groups, and other organizations; and is responsible for the running and maintaining of traveling movie houses (set up in large trucks) which go to the most remote regions and show films to people who often have never seen such things before.

We have often been led to believe that, under Castro, Cubans are exposed only to "propaganda" art in order to win supporters for the government. Quite to the contrary, art and culture in Cuba flourish in many and varied forms. While there is an emphasis on the social function of art and literature, this has never been so strong as to suppress creativity, and innovation and experimentation occur in all areas of art and culture. Cuban culture today is characterized by the determined attempt to create new forms, new media, new languages which can better reflect Cuban reality and meet Cuban needs. In the past, Cuban cultural expression was painfully derivative and imitative; today it stands by itself as a testimony to its creators and its public.

Epilogue

What the Future Holds

While the study of Cuba's past should help to clarify Cuba's present, it is inevitable that we end up with questions as well as answers. The biggest question is, how long will Cuban society as it is now constituted survive? The answer will depend on many factors. Most important, perhaps, is the attitude of the Cubans themselves. Will they continue to support the Cuban socialist government with the same energy and enthusiasm they have up to now? There seems every reason to believe that this will continue, for there is no denying that in purely human terms life is immeasurably better for the average Cuban today than it was prior to 1959. Those several million Cubans who had nothing before, who lived in poverty and ignorance, are not likely to provoke or support a change in the system which has brought them a more humane way of life.

It is true, of course, that not all those who are dissatisfied or who oppose the present regime have left, and there is little doubt that the more militant among them will periodically attempt acts of opposition or sabotage. But even those Cubans who were relatively well off before the revolution, and who may today feel regrets at the changes of the past decade or so, have nevertheless chosen to remain there. Conversations with nonrevolutionary Cubans still living on the island reveal that, despite some dissatisfactions, they have a strong patriotic sense and have recognized that life is better today for the vast majority of Cubans.

A second factor to consider is Cuba's relations with the socialist world, for to date the Cuban government has had to depend in large measure on the willingness of the Soviet Union, China, and other socialist countries to trade with it and provide professionals and technicians to tide Cuba over its scarcity of commodities and skilled personnel. There is no doubt that any large country, Russia or the United States, attaches strings to its trade agreements, and the question involves the extent to which Cuba can and will be bound by the strings linking it to its new trading partners, and the extent to which it cannot and will not do so. Until Cuba is economically self-sufficient—therefore strong—a certain amount of compromising will no doubt be necessary, but how far that will go remains to be seen.

Another major factor involves the relations between Cuba and the United States. While relations—diplomatic and trade—between the two countries were completely severed in 1961, there are individuals in the United States who feel that it would be beneficial to the business community for regularized trading with Cuba to be resumed. With the thaw in relations between the United States and China, one wonders if perhaps the United States might approach its relations with Cuba in the same way. Whether the Cuban government would be eager to reestablish such contacts with this country is open to question.

It is important further to examine Cuba's relationship to the rest of Latin America. In May, 1972, the OAS voted to reconsider the question of Cuba, which had been expelled from membership in that organization in 1962. In recent years Chile and Peru have on their own recognized Cuba and established normal relations with the socialist government there. Many other South American republics evidently wish now to rebuild commercial and diplomatic ties with Cuba, recognizing the mutual benefits of such arrangements. The degree to which such continental relations may grow will also affect the direction and longevity of the present Cuban system. In trying to predict, we can only see the extent to which Cuba's future is linked to that of the rest of the continent, and the future of Latin America is linked just as closely to Cuba's.

How, then, can we evaluate today's Cuba? Those who fear "Communism" claim that Cuba has never been as badly off as it is under the present government. Those on the other side claim the opposite. But the facts seem to speak for themselves. True, Cuban socialism has brought with it some control of the press; true, freedom of speech is not extended to those who openly express hostility to the regime; true, the elections which Castro promised in 1959 have never been held. These truths must be balanced against the achievements of the Cuban regime, against the realities of Cuban life today.

It may be true that men and women do not live by bread alone, but the spirit cannot flourish if the stomach is empty. The fact is that today's Cuba has produced a life-style for its people which is light years removed from the misery-ridden society of the 1950s. Cubans today eat well, have free health care available whenever they need it, have every opportunity to study and advance at no cost, receive ample and regular salaries, and are exposed to and participate in a broad variety of cultural and leisure time activities.

Despite these realities, people have often wondered just how popular the government is, since elections, the traditional gauge of popularity in the United States, have not been available to the Cuban population since 1959. Although in the earliest period of the revolution its leaders spoke of future elections, Cuba's move into socialism changed their policies. In theory, at least, a socialist society continues to elect local leadership in communities, factories, schools, and other institutions. Thus, in today's Cuba, students, teachers, professors, and workers in offices, factories, and farms all elect their leaders and representatives. The bulk of the Cuban population is not disturbed by the fact that national elections are not held. Past experience has taught them that the electoral system as they knew it brought in one corrupt government after another, and the present situation—in which the Cuban militia comprises the majority of the people, and is armed at all times—seems to indicate that ordinary Cubans now hold a much stronger weapon than a ballot. To date there has been no attempt by Cubans on the life of any of the top leaders, including Castro.

Socialist Cuba, then, seems to be here to stay. If Cuba is allowed to pursue its national destiny without interference by other countries, if helped and advised when it requests assistance but left to make its own decisions, there is no reason to believe that the present system will change radically. The Cuban people seem to have agreed to the brand of socialism that exists there, and because Cuba is a sovereign nation with a population well equipped to make its own choices, its future should be left securely in the hands of its people. Any other approach could be disastrous, not only for Cuba but for the rest of the world.

Index

About the Author

Victoria Ortiz grew up in Mexico, the United States, and Europe. She received a bachelor's degree in French and Spanish literature from Barnard College and attended Brandeis University as a Woodrow Wilson Fellow. She has worked as a tour guide at the United Nations, a caseworker for various social agencies, and a high school and college teacher of French, Spanish, and Latin-American literature. She has traveled extensively in Europe, Asia, and Latin America, and visited Cuba during the summer of 1963.

Ms. Ortiz translated Che Guevara's *Reminiscences of the Cuban Revolutionary War*, which was published in 1968, and many shorter works which have appeared in anthologies of Latin-American and Mexican-American literature. She lives in New York and is currently working toward a doctorate in the field of French and Spanish Caribbean literature at the City University of New York.